Between Two Worlds *An Architectural History of Emmanuel College Cambridge*

Jeremy Musson
with photographs by Will Pryce

Between Two Worlds

An Architectural History of Emmanuel College Cambridge

SCALA

To Sophie, my wife of 25 years

First published in 2017 by
Scala Arts & Heritage Publishers Ltd
10 Lion Yard · Tremadoc Road · London SW4 7NQ, UK
www.scalapublishers.com

In association with
Emmanuel College Cambridge
Cambridge CB2 3AP

ISBN 978-1-78551-078-6

Project managed by Coralie Hepburn
Edited by Linda Schofield
Designed and typeset in Verdigris by Dalrymple
Printed and bound in China

10 9 8 7 6 5 4 3 2 1

Frontispiece: Detail of the stonework and carving on the centrepiece of the Wren-designed Chapel and Gallery range.
Front cover: Wren's Cloister opening into Front Court (see pp. 54–55).
Back cover: The 2009–11 Kilburn Nightingale Library (see p. 158)

Contents

Preface

Enter Emmanuel College from a busy Cambridge shopping street and you are met by one of the most arresting and beautiful sights in the city: the perfect proportions of our Chapel, designed by Christopher Wren for a far-sighted Master in the seventeenth century and framed within an elegant Cloister and the formality of Front Court. Step through the arches to the right of the Chapel and you enter another world. Now you are in the Paddock, an unusual, informal and exceptionally attractive space where (subject to the weather or time of year) you are likely to find students relaxing in the sunshine, playing tennis or watching the processions of ducks and ducklings for which Emmanuel is so famous.

That mix of precise formality with informal, hospitable space is a hallmark of Emmanuel and helps explain our much-valued reputation as 'the friendly college'. To reach the Paddock, you will have entered by the Porters' Lodge, where there is always a warm welcome. As you explore the College you will bump into all manner of people – Fellows, undergraduates, graduates, staff and visitors – who relish being here and whose affection for this place is manifest.

This relationship between people and place is something that has intrigued and inspired me all my life. When I worked for the National Trust I was constantly reminded that each place has its own spirit, born of its history, special qualities, stories and, of course, people. That often indefinable but instantly recognisable spirit is what people love and remember about a place, and builds their relationship with it.

At Emmanuel we started trying to capture our spirit of place soon after I arrived in 2013. Ideas came from all directions: our Puritan foundations, which established a meritocratic and philanthropic element from the beginning; our hard-working, no-nonsense culture that has contributed to our high ranking in the academic tables for over two decades; and the inspiration provided by the sheer beauty of our buildings and gardens. And there are many contrasts: between formality and informality, [previous pages] *Emmanuel College seen from the north-west; the main elevation was rebuilt to designs of James Essex in the 1770s, and on the left-hand side is the 1950s' kitchen range, designed by Robert Hurd.*

[below] *Dame Fiona Reynolds was elected the first female Master of Emmanuel in 2012.*

buildings and open spaces, new and old, academic pursuit and relaxation; and between a sense of tradition and our determination to embrace the future. These ideas shape who we are, how we make decisions and the values we hold.

Out of this exercise came a desire to ensure that everyone who cares about Emmanuel should have, readily to hand, a beautifully illustrated narrative of our history and all that we celebrate about the College. We are delighted that the architectural historian Jeremy Musson took up the opportunity with such relish and persuaded the brilliant photographer, Will Pryce, to work with him on the book. What you see here is the product of their partnership, which included a detailed revisiting of our archives and many other sources to tell the richest possible story of Emmanuel's foundation and evolution.

We have widened Emmanuel's story to describe what went on before the College was founded. This was, to me, a riveting yet little-known element when I arrived as Master. But it has a profound influence on the place today, because there has been remarkable continuity since the site was occupied by friars of the Dominican Order who were living in Cambridge by 1238. Our pond is their fish pond, our dining hall their chapel, and it seems likely that the footprint of Front Court reflects the arrangement of the Dominican buildings. When the site was selected by Sir Walter Mildmay for his new college, to improve the training of preachers for the Church of England, he was pleased to adapt what was left of a group of eminently suitable buildings, abandoned when the priory was dissolved by Henry VIII in 1538.

Having established that teaching and learning have been going on here since at least 1238, Jeremy's text takes us, century by century, through Emmanuel's story. Each century is marked by new or rearranged buildings, by wider political and economic forces, including those within Cambridge University, and by colourful personalities, all of whom left their mark on the College. We learn of the characters who led change: the founder Mildmay himself and his descendants the Fanes and Earls of [following pages] *The Hall, set for a special dinner. Despite its eighteenth-century character, the Hall was created in the 1580s within the walls of the former priory church. The panelling is from the late seventeenth century, while the ceiling plasterwork was designed by James Essex in the 1760s.*

Westmorland, who have continued to support the College over the centuries; John Harvard, the modest pupil-priest who left with many fellow Emmanuel men to found the colonies in New England; William Sancroft, who commissioned Christopher Wren to design the Chapel as he left the College to become Dean of St Paul's and eventually Archbishop of Canterbury; the gregarious Richard Farmer, who is credited with bringing Samuel Johnson to Emmanuel on his sole visit to Cambridge; the multidimensional scientists Thomas Young (of wave theory) and the Revd Samuel Phear, one of the founders of the Cavendish Laboratory; and the determined and ambitious Edward Welbourne, one of the longest-serving recent Masters.

We learn too of the many architects and idealists who have shaped this place: Christopher Wren, who worked here before he was commissioned to build the new St Paul's Cathedral after the Fire of London; James Essex's sensitive improvements to our beautiful dining hall and Front Court; Charles Humfrey's addition of New Court; Arthur Blomfield's Master's Lodge (now demolished); William Fawcett's Hostel and John Loughborough Pearson's additions to it and construction of Emmanuel House; and Leonard Stokes's Lecture Rooms, now the Library, and elegant North Court. In the twentieth century we added Tom Hancock's South Court and the new Master's Lodge, Michael and Patty Hopkins's remarkable Queen's Building and a modern extension of the Library by Kilburn Nightingale.

We hear of the prescient purchase from Jesus College of the elegant Park Terrace buildings in 1983, extending the College southwards, and we also learn of the things that (fortunately) did not happen: plans by Sir James Burrough or James Essex for a radical reshaping of Front Court in the eighteenth century; Stokes's designs for three large buildings in the Paddock, gently but firmly rejected by the Fellows; and Arthur Blomfield's proposal to knock down and rebuild the Chapel in the nineteenth century. Thank goodness – sometimes – for a lack of money.

But above all we learn about the delicate balance between continuity and change, maintaining always those characteristics that make Emmanuel special and the people who have nurtured it. Those people in the late twentieth and early twenty-first centuries include recent Masters: immediately after Lord St John of Fawsley the College was led by Professor Shôn Ffowcs Williams, the noted engineer responsible for reductions in the noise levels of supersonic flights; and Lord Wilson of Dinton, the former Cabinet Secretary. And, since 1976, the College has admitted women, with the first female undergraduates arriving in 1979. While I am honoured to be the first female Master of Emmanuel, I stand in the footsteps of many remarkable women. These include Professor Susan Rankin, Emmanuel's first female professorial Fellow; Moira Wallace, one of our first cohort of undergraduates who became the first female Provost of Oriel College Oxford in 2013 after a distinguished career in the civil service; the first female Emmanuel graduate to become a Life Peer, Elizabeth Berridge; and since 2010 our first female Member of Parliament, Nicola Blackwood.

Emmanuel gets into your bones: it is an easy place to fall in love with, and it has shaped all our lives. I am enormously grateful to Jeremy for capturing it so beautifully and empathetically in this wonderful book.

Dame Fiona Reynolds *Master*

Introduction: A Welcome

Emmanuel College Cambridge was founded by Sir Walter Mildmay in 1584.[1] The College occupies a significant place in the development of the University, and the city, and has a place in international history through its role in the idealistic New England settlements of the 1630s as well as in the scientific advances of the twentieth century. This book traces the physical and intellectual identity of the College through the story of its diverse collection of buildings and the people behind them.

The story of buildings is always revealing, even if they mean different things to different people. In a debate about the bomb-damaged House of Commons in 1943, Winston Churchill said: 'We shape our buildings and afterwards our buildings shape us'.[2] Emmanuel's buildings – of different ages, uses and textures – have been shaped by founders, Fellows and Masters, donors and dons. In turn, the buildings have helped shape the identity, spirit and reputation of the College and of generations of students since its foundation.

There are longer histories embedded in these structures. Emmanuel was built up on the bones of a thirteenth-century Dominican priory, which had its own role in University teaching and theology. From its 1584 royal founding charter, Emmanuel was given a clear view of its future role as 'A perpetual College of sacred theology, science, philosophy and good arts in the University of Cambridge'. This is clearly echoed in the oath sworn by new Fellows today, to 'endeavour to the utmost of my power to promote the honour and interests of the College' as a place of education and learning.[3]

Naturally, many things have changed since Emmanuel was founded. The College is an historic institution that began life on the outskirts of Cambridge, but today is well within the city (technically a town until 1951), hard against offices, shops, coffee bars, pubs and a bus station. Yet inside the College gates is a private, reflective world and a sense of Emmanuel's rural origins still lingers among the tall trees and open spaces that are every bit as important as the buildings in which the College is housed.

[previous pages] *The Chapel, facing east, lit for evensong. The eastern orientation of the new Chapel, designed by Christopher Wren and built during the 1670s at the invitation of William Sancroft, was a symbolic change of course for the 'Puritan' foundation.*

These buildings and gardens provide a constant resource and are as vital to the experience of students today as they were in earlier centuries.[4] The green spaces of Emmanuel are evidently of defining importance to the nature and character of the College, as a place and as a community. They have been cultivated, planted, shaped and tended in different ways over the centuries, and include courts, gardens and a park-like Paddock. Early College gardens were planted to provide fruit and vegetables for the College household, but as needs and techniques of provisioning changed, they became places that students and Fellows could use for recreation or to reflect on their studies among peaceful walks and 'Closes' (in the sense of 'enclosures').

These layers are never entirely separate and their coexistence informs every part of a college where the past is literally built into the present. A section of one of these ancient walls of thirteenth-century origin serves to anchor the adventurous 2010 Library extension, a timber and glass layer added to a 1970s' wing that makes use of the latest environmentally friendly construction methods and provides study spaces for twenty-first-century students.

[opposite] *A monument to an Emmanuel scholar, Henry Skaiffe, who died in 1711, within the Cloister designed by Wren.*

The first visual impression of Emmanuel, from the street, is also atypical for an historic Cambridge college. The smooth, pale, ashlar stone of its eighteenth-century entrance range is distinctive but more discreet than imposing, perhaps reminiscent of a grand private residence. It would be easy to imagine this building in a park between clumps of oaks, overlooking a lawn running down to a lake. Yet the taller wings at either end of the range offer hints of a different world within the wider embrace of its walls.

Stepping through the central archway, with the Porters' Lodge unobtrusively to one side, visitors find themselves in a covered cloister with views over an immaculate lawn framed by eighteenth-century ashlar elevations: today's Front Court. This experience of passing through a restricted opening into an expansive space is one of many such contrasting aesthetic experiences the College offers. Opposite the entrance stands one of the city's late seventeenth-century architectural gems: part of a classical set piece designed by Christopher Wren and commissioned in the 1660s by an imaginative Master of Emmanuel, William Sancroft.

This range consists of an arcaded walk or Cloister, with a Gallery over, intersecting with a pedimented and decorated Corinthian 'temple-front' centrepiece. By the time Wren produced the design, Sancroft had become Dean of St Paul's, where he was also instrumental in Wren's appointment to design the new cathedral there. In this and in many other ways, singular threads of national history are entwined with Emmanuel's reticent courts and gardens.

[following pages] *The enclosed grounds of Emmanuel contain many trees, following a tradition established by the founding Master, Laurence Chaderton: (left) looking towards the Chapel, (above right) towards the Fellows' Garden across the pond, and (below right) Chapman's Garden.*

Henricus Skaiffe,
Natus Glattoniæ, in
Comitat: Huntingdon.
hujus Coll: A.B.
et Scholaris
Discipulus,
Obijt, Sept: 30
1711.

The Chapel was a symbol of a new start for Emmanuel. A college is a curiously active and evolving microcosm in which the pressure of the rising generation engages directly and indirectly with the learning and experience of the older, creating a palpable, organic tension. This mixing of the generations, which is inevitable, naturally produces its own kind of energy, familiar across all the 31 historic and modern colleges that make up the University of Cambridge, each of which must balance the demands of the future and the past.

Emmanuel's buildings were all built with a common intent to serve the collective needs of the College but ideas of what was necessary, practical and appropriate have shifted and evolved over time. The older buildings are not static but subject to additions and alterations, reflecting changing philosophies about past ages. Today, the rate of visible modification may have slowed, but the energetic flutter of technological advances

Questioning minds: a figure of a seated Buddha (Sakyamuni Buddha or historical Buddha) on the landing approach to the Gallery, with Wren's richly decorated elevation seen through the window. The figure was the gift of Sir John Phear (Chief Justice of Ceylon [modern day Sri Lanka]) to his brother George, Master of Emmanuel, who gave it to the College in 1895.

creates a surreal touch that might well have appealed to the seventeenth-century philosophers of Emmanuel.

As anyone who has experience of an historic college will know, what makes these places so rich is the people who inhabit the buildings. A College is above all a 'society'. Indeed generations of dedicated Masters, Fellows, Senior Tutors and Bursars have played an important part in stamping Emmanuel's identity and also ensuring its modern success, and its future. This College has also been fortunate in its later twentieth-century Masters, several of whom have come from outside the world of academia and have contributed much to the feel of the College and its society in their own way.

At Emmanuel, there are those who devote their careers to scholarship, and those who support the wider life of the College: its administrators, porters, housekeepers and those who run the kitchen and halls, and who care for the students, gardens and the buildings, all of whom make it such a memorable place of welcome and hospitality. The whole of this busy 'society' gives Emmanuel its meaning, including its many birds of passage who take with them a lifelong imprint of this place, and those who dwell here longer. They all leave behind them the buildings and the grounds, which provide us with marks on a map that help to navigate the broader cultural history and topography of the College.

From Front Court, the buildings unexpectedly spread out into green spaces behind. Beyond the Chapel and Gallery range stands the 'Paddock', which has been known by that name since at least the end of the nineteenth century. Ringed with trees, it is loosely framed by buildings that are clearly the result of incremental additions rather than a formal grand plan. Old Court (the long, brick building facing the Paddock), which was built in the mid-1630s to provide sets of rooms for students, forms part of the Paddock's western boundary.

Close to this (running to the east) lies the stately brick-and-stone Library, which began life as Lecture Rooms in 1909. Between the Library and Old Court can be glimpsed the modern massing of the 1960s' accommodation block: South Court. Its pale brick-and-stone-clad walls are part of the twentieth-century evolution of the College, now overtaken by the vertical timber and glass lines of the 2009–11 Library extension that belong to the twenty-first century. To the east of the Paddock lie the nineteenth-century Hostel and Emmanuel House, which help frame the open spaces in a self-consciously picturesque manner.

In summer, tennis nets are raised on the grass of the Paddock, and throughout term groups of students can be found on this ancient green space, once the enclosure of a thirteenth-century Dominican priory. Moorhens and ducks inhabit the fringes of the fine serpentine pond first dug to provide fish for the monastic table, then maintained as a long, canal-like presence, before its rather utilitarian shape was reworked into curves in the mid-1960s.

Visible to the south of the Paddock are the varied and leafy gardens of Park Terrace, handsome south-facing Regency houses (two terraces, two villas and a pair of semi-detached houses in between) acquired by the College in 1983 to add new accommodation. To the north rise the stone gables of North Court, completed in 1914. There are more modern landmarks in this architectural topography, notably, for instance, the 1995 stone-and-glass Queen's Building, which lies alongside the Fellows' Garden. Built in the same Ketton stone as the Wren-designed Chapel, this combined lecture room and concert hall is a rare modern celebration of stone architecture.

The high note of the Fellows' Garden is its magnificent, cathedral-like plane tree (*Platanus orientalis*) planted in the very early 1800s. The canopy of its spreading branches is large enough to define a stage for theatrical performances or to enclose a twinkling room of tea lights at a May Ball. Tucked into a discreet corner of the garden is an open-air bathing pool dating from 1745 and still used today. This is one of the few such college pools to have survived, bringing with it a suggestion of long-enjoyed summer pleasures.

Emmanuel's architecture is demonstrably less formal than the grand courts of some of the older colleges, but it is not without formality. Visitors will note the almost diminutive scale elevation of the Gallery and Cloister designed by Wren, which frames Front Court. This has informed later developments and has been a significant factor in preserving a human scale

that could easily have been lost in the eighteenth or nineteenth centuries. Although it feels intimate, Emmanuel is, in numbers, one of the largest of the middle-sized colleges, and sits among the top ranks of the academic league tables (it has been in the top five since 1998).

This book is essentially a journey through Emmanuel and its buildings, particularly from the foundation onwards, giving a flavour of the strong personalities and overall character of the place in different periods. More can be found on the rich and complex narrative of Emmanuel, its intellectual life, people and estates, in Sarah Bendall, Christopher Brooke and Patrick Collinson's comprehensive *A History of Emmanuel College, Cambridge* (1999), and the many scholarly writings of Frank Stubbings, including the enjoyable *Forty-Nine Lives* (1983). Here, we take this journey in large part visually through Will Pryce's perceptive new photography, taken especially for this publication, which helps to reveal a complex architectural story of a living institution, and takes us to the heart of the historic, social and aesthetic character of Emmanuel.

[opposite and above]
The Parlour, or historic Combination Room, set for Fellows to withdraw for the dessert course from the formal Hall. The room was created for this purpose in the 1580s and was refitted in the 1760s; the colour scheme was introduced by Master Lord St John Fawsley in the 1990s, as a fitting setting for Emmanuel's finest eighteenth-century portraits.

1

The House That Came Before

To understand the built form that Emmanuel took on its foundation, it is important to have a sense of the site as it was when its founder, Sir Walter Mildmay, acquired it in November 1583.[1] For then it included some buildings that had belonged to the Dominican Order before passing into private hands after the Dissolution of the Monasteries in the 1530s. At least one part of the priory's buildings appears to have been converted into a private residence, although which part of the former priory is not known. The priory was also still remembered by the name of the street that outlived it, 'Preachers' Street' (which later became St Andrew's Street).

The Dominican Order was founded in 1216 by a Castilian priest, Dominic Guzman (canonised – in 1234 – as St Dominic after his death in 1221). Dominicans followed the Rule of St Augustine, taking vows of obedience, chastity and poverty, with a dedicated mission to preach, but were expected to live out in the world, so they settled in towns and cities.[2] They were known in England as the 'Black Friars' because of their black capes and hoods. As the Order grew, Dominicans were associated with many universities, founding houses in famous centres of learning such as Paris and Bologna. They arrived in Oxford in 1221 and in Cambridge by 1238, where they settled in the parish of St Andrew, just outside the Barnwell Gate, and remained there for more than three centuries (there were some 55 Dominican priories in England by the early sixteenth century).[3]

Royal patronage helped the Dominicans flourish in both Cambridge and Oxford. In 1238, Henry III made a gift of three oaks for the building of the Cambridge priory church and in 1240 an adjoining lane was closed to enlarge the cemetery. A new road (Preachers' Lane, later Emmanuel Street) was also created. During the 1240s Henry III sent money and more oaks for the priory church, which may have begun with the choir, and the nave built in stages. The priory church was completed in the 1280s.[4] By 1279, the Black Friars' house occupied:

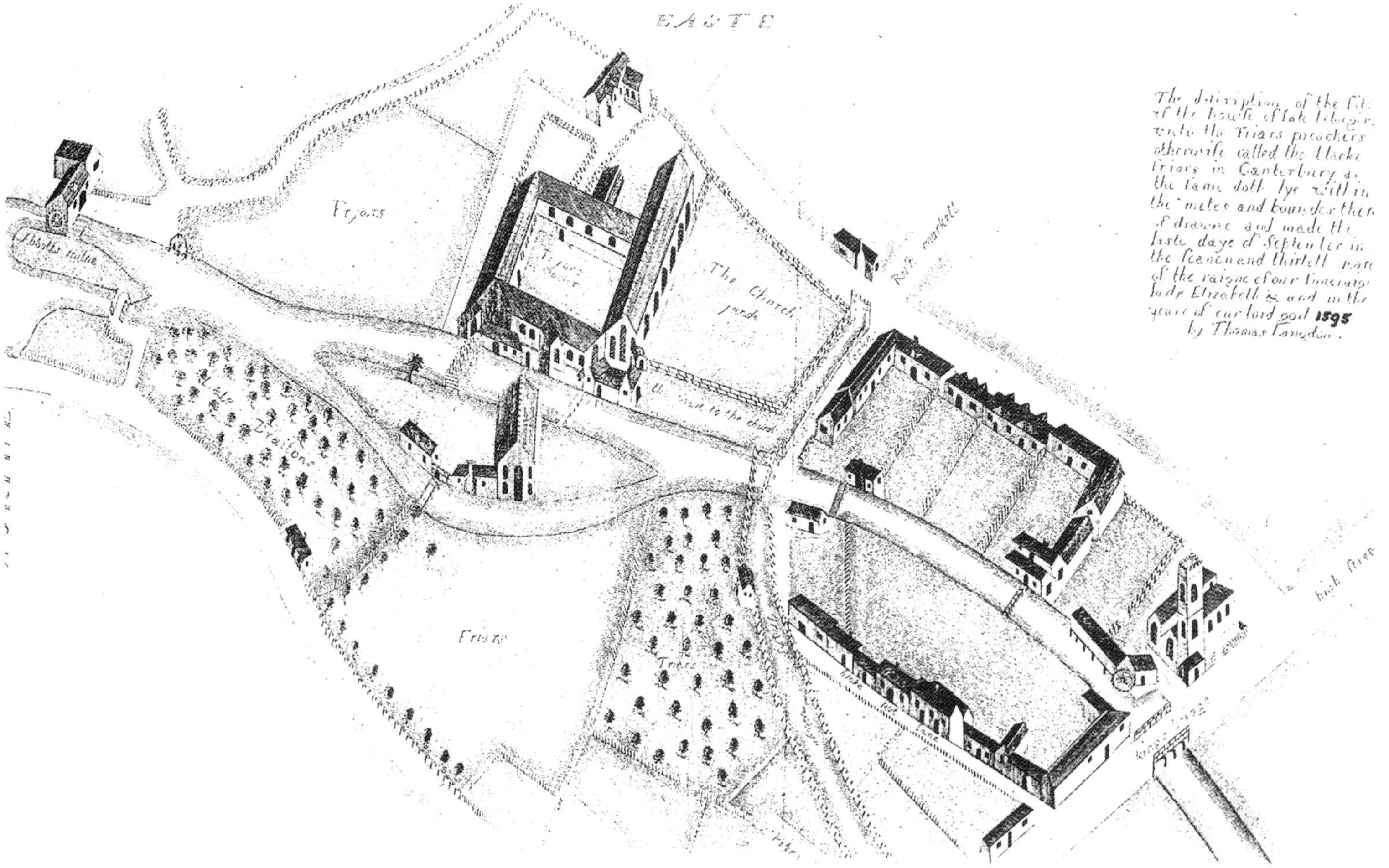

[above] *A 1595 depiction of the Black Friars' house in Canterbury by Thomas Langdon (as engraved in 1792 by Sir Egerton Bridges), which illustrates an overall arrangement that may in general terms have been similar to the Cambridge Black Friars' house, with a long, unaisled thirteenth-century priory church with no tower and a continuous long choir.*

[previous pages] *Portrait of Henry III: detail from a thirteenth-century depiction of his coronation, by an unknown artist. The king was one of the most important patrons of the Dominican houses in both Cambridge and Oxford.*

eight acres and more in length and breadth; on that site there used to be divers dwellings in which many people dwelt who were wont to pay geld and aid to the town; now the friars hold the land in perpetual alms from their purchases and the gifts of many donors.[5]

Edward I stayed for two days as a guest at the priory in 1297.[6]

Dominican priories tended to follow a compact physical pattern, surrounded by enclosures for livestock and the cultivation of herbs, fruit and vegetables.[7] One of the great survivals of the monastic era of the Emmanuel site is the long pond in the 'Paddock', which was probably the original fish pond, a source of food, continuing as a water feature but only made serpentine in the 1960s. There was a long-naved church, the building adapted as the College Hall in the 1580s, as evidenced by traces of a nave altar discovered in the Parlour during eighteenth-century works, 'very apparent near the present fire-place',[8] with perhaps some hint of painted decoration and the west window visible in David Loggan's (1634–1692) bird's-eye view of the College published in 1690.[9] There would also have been a long, distinct choir where the friars could celebrate mass and sing the daily offices (the nave and choir separated by a walkway). Ranges of the adjoining cloister usually contained the refectory and the dormitory, which provided beds in the centre and places for study along the walls in 'carrels' lit by windows.[10] A prior's lodgings and a chapter house for meetings were important features of priories: a chapter house would have stood at the east of the cloister. Archaeological investigations in the mid-1990s suggested a guest house stood to the north-east (on the site of the present Queen's Building).[11] The Cambridge Black Friars' establishment was clearly large: extensive enough to host a sitting of Parliament from 9 September to 7 October 1388.[12]

The main buildings are presumed to have occupied the north-western corner of the plot, around the thirteenth-century church, later the Hall range of Emmanuel.[13] Modern surveys suggest that today's Front Court encloses the approximate position of the medieval cloister. The presence of medieval elements in the west range, as recorded by Loggan, also hints at the cloister being to the south. It is equally possible that the 1580s' Founder's Range made use of earlier foundations and walls. The current Chapel may indeed stand where the former chapter house existed by analogy with other sites such as the Oxford Black Friars.[14] The prior's lodgings were likely to have been part of the main cloister.

The thirteenth century was the heyday of the order and from this time the Cambridge Black Friars' house was considered

Dominican friars wearing black-and-white robes, depicted dining with Sir Geoffrey Luttrell, from the Luttrell Psalter (1320–40).

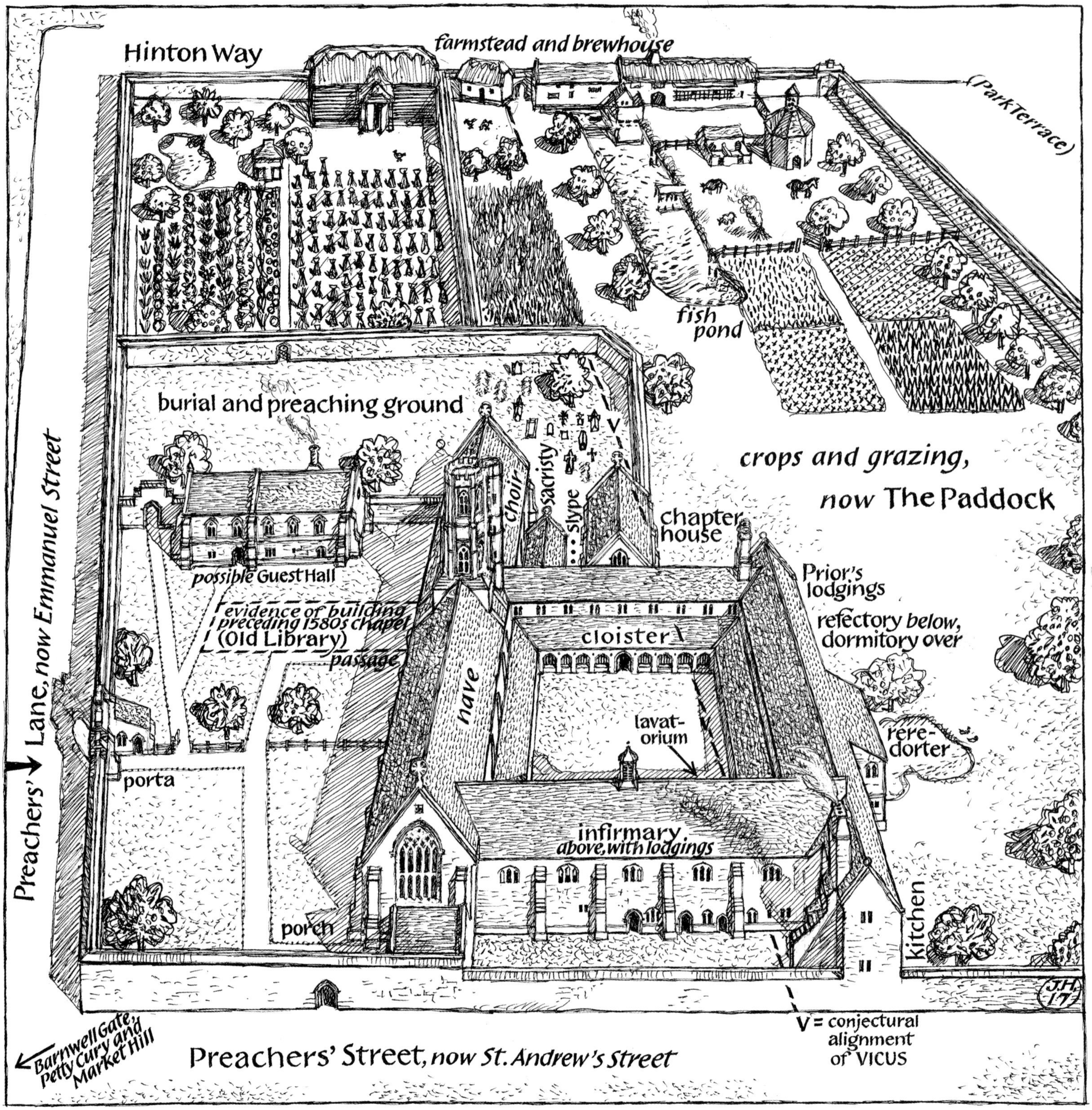

A conjectural reconstruction of how the Cambridge Black Friars might have looked, in a new drawing by Jon Harris. This is based on comparisons with plans of other Dominican priories and such evidence as can be drawn from surviving medieval fragments, Frank Stubbings's researches on the priory church, and details suggested by Loggan's bird's-eye view of the College, published in 1690.

'second only to the Oxford house in the system of Dominican education'.[15] In 'Lives of the Brethren' (*Vitae Fratrum*), written in the late 1250s, one Brother Seyer was remembered as 'well known for his life and learning and a lector in the University of Cambridge'.[16] That these mendicant houses had a strong intellectual identity cannot be doubted; John Caius, re-founder of Gonville and Caius College in 1557, recalled how like colleges they were in character before the Dissolution.[17] Together with the Franciscans, the Dominicans had a strong hand in developing Cambridge's Faculty of Theology, with Dominican William Ringesham becoming its first Doctor of Divinity around 1262.[18]

There were about 70 Dominicans resident at the end of the thirteenth century and the Cambridge Black Friars found a major patron in Alice, wife of Robert de Vere, 5th Earl of Oxford, who helped them extend their landholding and buildings (including the church, work that was completed by 1286).[19] The Cambridge house was formally named a *studium generale* in 1318 and produced many scholars including, it is traditionally suggested, Robert Holcot, whose *Postilla super librum Sapientiae*, an important commentary on the Book of Wisdom, is thought to be based on lectures given at Cambridge.[20] In 1383, John de Bromyard, one of Cambridge's Dominican theologians, was elected Chancellor of the University.[21]

The priory church must have been elaborately fitted up: there has been a suggestion that the famous painted retable now at Thornham Parva, Suffolk, may possibly have originally been here (the retable was probably made for the church of one of the major Dominican houses in East Anglia, although Norwich or Thetford have been considered more likely).[22] The Cambridge priory church was certainly a popular focus for pilgrims, particularly for its statue of Our Lady of Grace first mentioned in 1505.[23]

Dominicans at their desks: detail of a fresco from the cycle of Forty Illustrious Members of the Dominican Order, *1352, by Tommaso da Modena (1326–1379), from the Chapter Hall of the Dominicans, the Episcopal Seminary (formerly the convent of St Nicholas), Treviso, Italy.*

The Thornham Parva retable, an outstanding example of a Dominican church fitting, depicting St Dominic and St Peter Martyr in the outer panels in the robes of the Dominican Order. This is Britain's largest and most complete medieval altarpiece, possibly created in a Norwich workshop in the 1330s for a major priory church, most probably Thetford or Norwich itself, although Cambridge has also been considered a potential location.

It was once thought that this might be the carved figure now in the Catholic Church of Our Lady and the English Martyrs, reputed to have been discovered 'in the grounds of or in the walls of the college' in around 1850, and presented to Cambridge's pre-eminent Catholic church in the very early 1900s.[24] In 1538, John Hilsey, the new head of the Dominican Order in England, ordered the new prior to seek Lord Cromwell's permission to remove a figure of Our Lady from people's sight because they could not bear 'sych eydollatrye'.[25] But this debate was a sign of the times, because right up until the Reformation the house was the recipient of generous bequests from laymen: for example, in 1506 a doctor, Henry Rudde, gave 20 marks for 'the peynting of the ix ordrys of aungelis'.[26]

In 1526, Robert Buckenham (or Buckenam) was made prior and was one of the chief opponents of the Protestant reformer, Hugh Latimer. When Buckenham fled the country, a correspondent of the Archbishop of Canterbury, Thomas Cranmer, wrote:

> *Dr. Buckenham is an exile from our parts; he is one who will do mischief wherever he is ... In his place is appointed one of like fame, like judgement, I will not say learning, by name Olyver ... at Cambridge they cry out that it is a disgrace that he, who knows nothing but cookery, should be set over others. There are at that convent many young men whom his authority will easily lead from the truth. Certainly he has never favoured higher learning, and old bottles cannot bear new wine.*[27]

Cranmer thought Prior William Oliver entirely unfit to manage the priory, but noted there were other 'men of good study, living, learning and judgement' among the friars.[28] One of these was probably the last prior, Gregory Dodds, who had studied at Cambridge and Louvain (in present-day Belgium), and was entirely sympathetic to the ideal of reform. He readily surrendered the house to the state commissioners in 1538.

The surrendered priory was put into the hands of William Standyssh, principal of St Nicholas's Hostel, to hold 'to the King's use'. When the commissioners arrived, the 'religious persons' and their servants were all 'dispersed and gone'. Furniture and other movables had been taken away at the first surrender and the house was to be left 'undefaced until the King's pleasure be further known'.[29]

The site and buildings came into the hands of Edward Elrington and Humfrey Metcalfe by 1544. Various structures seem to have been dismantled during the 1530s and 1540s (and stone and lead removed apparently for repairwork on the Old Schools, Great St Mary's and elsewhere).[30] In 1545 they conveyed the site and remaining buildings to 'William Shirwood, gent'.[31] According to Thomas Fuller, the seventeenth-century historian, the Shirwoods (sometimes spelt Sherwoods or Shyrwoods) made a dwelling house out of the former priory, which the family owned until 1581.[32]

Of the 16 friars who signed the surrender, some left and found their way to Rome, while most had clerical careers in the reformed Church of England. Some became leading reformers, such as John Scory, an admired preacher (a chaplain to Cranmer and Nicholas Ridley) who became Bishop of Rochester in 1551, and then in 1552, of Chichester.[33]

During the reign of Mary I, as a married man Scory is said to have conformed to the Catholic prohibition of married priests by sending away his unfortunate wife. After a period of exile in Emden in Lower Saxony (modern Germany) from 1544, and then Geneva, he returned to become Bishop of Hereford in 1559; he was one of the first bishops to be nominated by Elizabeth I.[34] Scory would have known Lord Burghley, Lord High Treasurer, and also corresponded in 1585 with Mildmay.[35] Scory died in 1585, so he lived long enough to hear talk about the foundation of the new College of Emmanuel, in some of the very buildings where he had once been a young friar sympathetic to Protestant reform.

Early sixteenth-century North Netherlandish painting depicting the interior of a Flemish Dominican church with the appearance of the Virgin Mary with the Child Jesus before assembled Dominicans during a Salve Regina procession (at the end of Compline). This image illustrates both the importance of Marian devotion and the familiar layout of a Dominican church, as the figures stand in the nave while the choir can be seen beyond the screen and walkway; elaborate nave altars can also be seen on either side of the entrance to the choir.

2

Mildmay's Acorn and His Oaks

Emmanuel was one man's dream. Elizabeth I's Chancellor of the Exchequer, Sir Walter Mildmay, had a single driving ambition: to found a college that would improve the intellectual quality of the English clergy. It was named, not after a saint, nor after the founder, but 'Emmanuel': literally, 'God with us'. It was designed to be a 'seed-bed' of theological learning.[1] As Mildmay was renowned for the clarity and eloquence of his speaking, the College was also intended to foster good preaching.

In practical terms, the Black Friars' site clearly lent itself to the creation of a college, with its enclosed land and amenities for exercise and retreat. Mildmay's civil servant's mind took pleasure in adapting an existing set of buildings to a purpose that in part stood for the replacement and reform of the old order (the street was still then known as 'Preachers' Street'). Some must have been usable right away, and it is tempting to suggest (as has often been done) that the desire to repurpose the former priory church building (and famous shrine for pilgrimages) to the non-religious function of College Hall was a deliberate act.

The November 1583 conveyance of the land described the property as:

> *all that the scite circuite ambulance and procincte of the late Priorye of Fryers Prechers commonlie called the Black Fryers w[ith]in the Towne of Cambri[d]ge … and all messuages houses buildings, barnes stables dovehouses orchardes gardens pondes waters lande and soile within the said scite … And all the walles of stone, brick or other thinge compassinge and enclosinge the said scite.*[2]

This makes it clear that the plot as it stood still retained a substantial core of buildings.

When Richard Lyne drew the first complete but not wholly accurate map of Cambridge in 1574, the former Black Friars appears as a diffuse group of long buildings at the north-western corner of a large enclosure on the edge of the town.[3] This site was acquired by one Robert Taylor from the previous owner, [previous pages] *The Hall, seen from the western cloister. The tall oriel window was originally part of the 1580s' Hall and allowed additional light to reach the High Table on the dais within; the Elizabethan roof structure remains behind the Georgian dormer windows.*

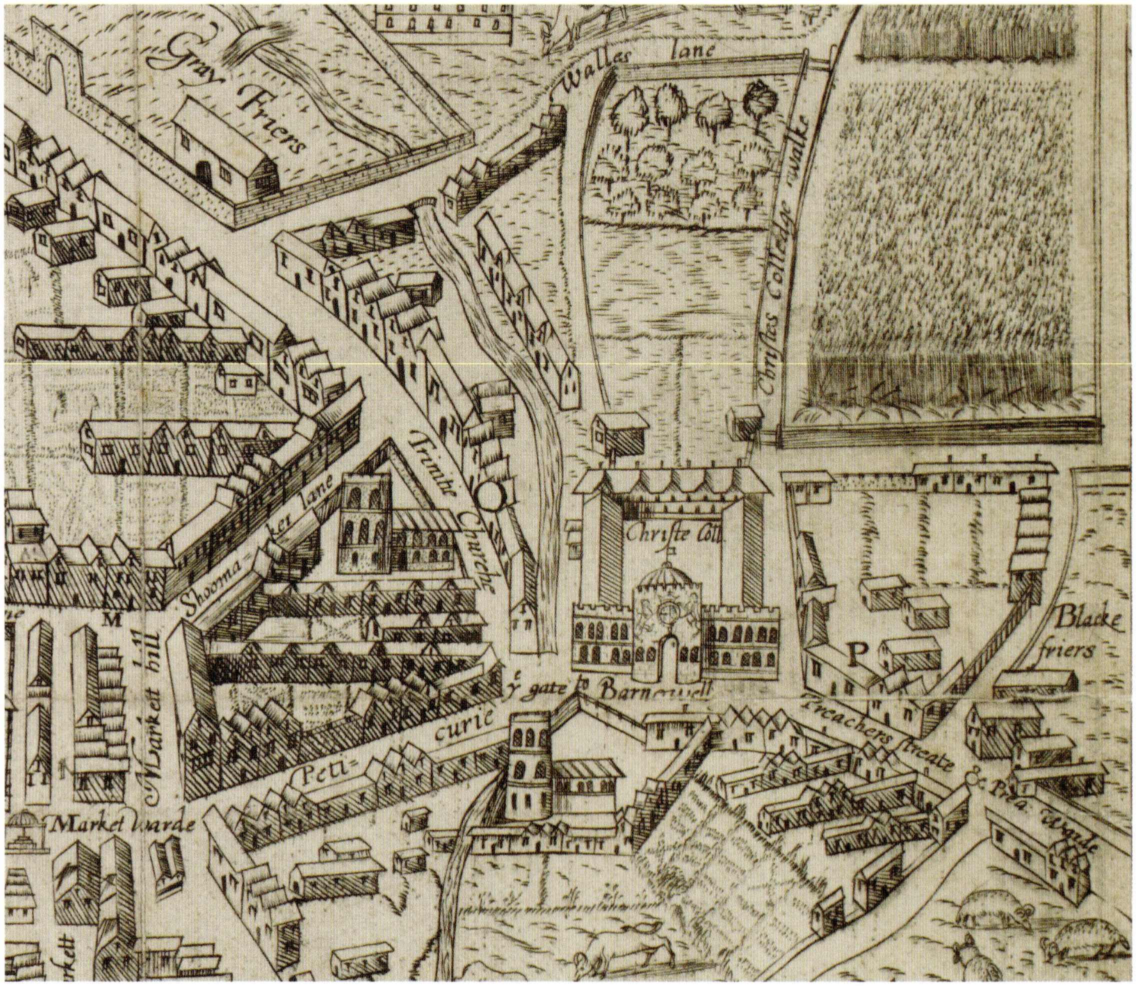

[right] *Richard Lyne's 1574 map of Cambridge showing the former Black Friars' buildings on the extreme eastern edge of the town, before they were acquired for the College in 1583. The depictions of the buildings are not considered very accurate.*

George Shirwood, in 1581. Within two years he sold the property to Richard Culverwell and Laurence Chaderton, who conveyed it to Sir Walter Mildmay – for £550 – in November 1583.

The memoir of the first Master, Laurence Chaderton, by William Dillingham referred to 'the ancient site of a community of preaching friars, almost buried in ruins', but judging by the long list of serviceable buildings mentioned in the title deed and the speed by which some were reoccupied, it was not really just 'ruins'.[4] Under Mildmay's direction, surviving buildings were prepared for use and new ones erected by mason Ralph Symons (or Simons).[5] Some buildings were ready by 1 November 1584 to receive the first 26 students who matriculated on that day.[6] It seems over 40 more had arrived by the end of 1586.[7]

Described as of 'Barkhamstedd in the Countie of Hartford Freemason', Symons probably first worked for Sir Edward Carey of Berkhampsted Place, Sir Walter Mildmay's brother-in-law. After Emmanuel, Symons was employed on the Great Hall at Trinity College and Second Court at St John's College, as well as the conversion of the former Franciscan friary buildings into Sidney Sussex College in the 1590s.[8] During the work on

[opposite] *Portrait of 1588 by an unknown artist of Sir Walter Mildmay (c.1523–1589), the founder of Emmanuel College in January 1584 and Elizabeth I's Chancellor of the Exchequer. The identity of the building seen through the window is not known.*

Effigies honoratissimi viri GVALTERI MILDMAII
VIRTVTE NON VI

Portrait by an unknown artist of Ralph Symons (or Simons), the mason who designed and oversaw the conversion of the former Dominican buildings into Emmanuel College. He also worked on St John's, Trinity and Sidney Sussex Colleges.

The initial 'E' from the Charter issued in 1584 by Elizabeth I for the founding of Emmanuel College, containing a portrait of the queen.

St John's, he appears to have lost a hand.[9] A mason-contractor by training, he was at the upper level of the artisan world. In his portrait in the College he is shown holding a large pair of engraved dividers, as if they were a sword handle, stressing perhaps an almost gentleman-like status.

In 1586, work had been carried out to the Fellows' Parlour at the east end of the Hall, with chambers above and alongside for the Master's lodgings. The Hall, fitted into the walls of the old Dominican priory church, received an entirely new roof structure (this survives above the eighteenth-century ceiling) and was already in use for dining by 1586.[10] It was a crucial place for the binding together of the College, and the 1584 statutes (modelled on those of Christ's College) state: 'since we desire them all to be united in one whole ... therefore we desire all the Fellows, the Scholars, and the pensioners of the aforesaid college to dine and sup in the common Hall thereof'.[11] The Hall was used for the dedication feast in December 1587, described by Sir Thomas Legge, Regius Professor of Civil Law and Vice-Chancellor in that year, as an event of 'joye and comforte'.[12]

During this period, an elegant new entrance was also created facing north onto Emmanuel Lane. Presumably designed by

[opposite] *A panel in the Hall opened to reveal the original 1580s' screens passage still* in situ.

An early record drawing (or possibly original design) in the College Archives thought to be of the 1580s' classically inspired entrance gate of Emmanuel with a somewhat eccentric depiction of masonry. It is missing the upper section of the gateway, which was a curved pediment and carried an inscription.

Symons, it was a crisp, pedimented structure, which spoke to the status and purpose of the place, and reflected the educated humanist values of Mildmay's generation (and can be compared to the *c.*1610 Nevile's Gate at Trinity, named after the College's Master, Thomas Nevile).[13] Emmanuel's gate bore a carved inscription: 'Sacrae Theologiae Studiosis posuit Gualterus Mildmaius A[nn]o D[omi]ni. 1584.'[14]

This gateway marked the entrance to a three-sided court, with a central broad path leading to the new Hall opposite. The Fellows' Parlour and Master's Lodge occupied the eastern part. Two lower wings to either side came northward from the Hall range: to the west lay the new Chapel, with additional chambers above, and to the east the kitchen, adapted from older buildings connected to the west end of the priory church. The kitchen itself formed another small court. The interior of the Hall appears to have always been one large volume with a buttery and pantry at the west end, behind a screens passage. Sections of the original 1580s' Hall screen survive behind the

The Elizabethan roof structure of the Hall, which remains above the Georgian ceiling.

[opposite] *A detail of David Loggan's bird's-eye view of the College, drawn in 1688 and published in 1690 in* Cantabrigia Illustrata, *showing the Hall, the kitchen range and the buttressed eastern range, which appears to have been an adaptation of a medieval building.*

F
B
D
C
E

A detail of an oil painting of the College based on Loggan's view, and thought to have been painted around 1700, showing some of the older buildings that had been adapted in the 1580s.

later seventeenth-century panelling, and suggest good robust woodwork with little superfluous decoration.

To the south of the Hall lay another open court with a substantial range to the west (on the equivalent line of today's entrance range), the visible buttresses showing that it was adapted from the former monastic buildings. In the late 1680s' bird's-eye view by David Loggan the ground floor seems rather blank on the northern end of the western range, which suggests it might have originally been a *cellarium*, or large, secure undercroft storeroom.

The southern range to this court was added in the 1580s and again probably followed the line of a previous building. Named the Founder's Building, it provided sets of accommodation over two storeys around three staircases, with a garret with dormers. It is shown (very little altered) in Loggan's view of the College made around a century later: stone-built, with plain mullioned windows and tall chimneys.

Symons's work at Emmanuel was clearly considered a success. When he was granted a 60-year lease on a house on the corner of Emmanuel Street and Preachers' Street in 1586, the lease made special reference to him as having 'shewed himself verie dilligent and carefull' in his work on Emmanuel.[15] As noted above, he went on to work on several colleges – Sidney Sussex, St John's and Trinity – thus helping to form the architectural identity of late Elizabethan and early Stuart Cambridge.

John Hamond's famous 1592 map of Cambridge shows Emmanuel as it was shortly after the completion of the first phase of works. It illustrates the two interlocking courts: one three-sided entrance court facing north, and the western range and Founder's Building forming another three-sided court (with the Hall in the middle) open to the east.[16] Hamond's map also suggests this was closed to the east by a low, single-storey covered walkway or possibly an arcade, allowing residents of the Founder's Building to reach the Hall and Chapel protected from the elements.

[opposite] *A detail of John Hamond's 1592 map of Cambridge, which shows Emmanuel College (bottom right) on the outskirts of the town. It shows the College shortly after the adaptation of the buildings of the former Dominican priory to serve as the newly founded Emmanuel. King's Chapel and Trinity and John's Colleges are all visible towards the top of the page.*

Clare Hall
Augustine Freers

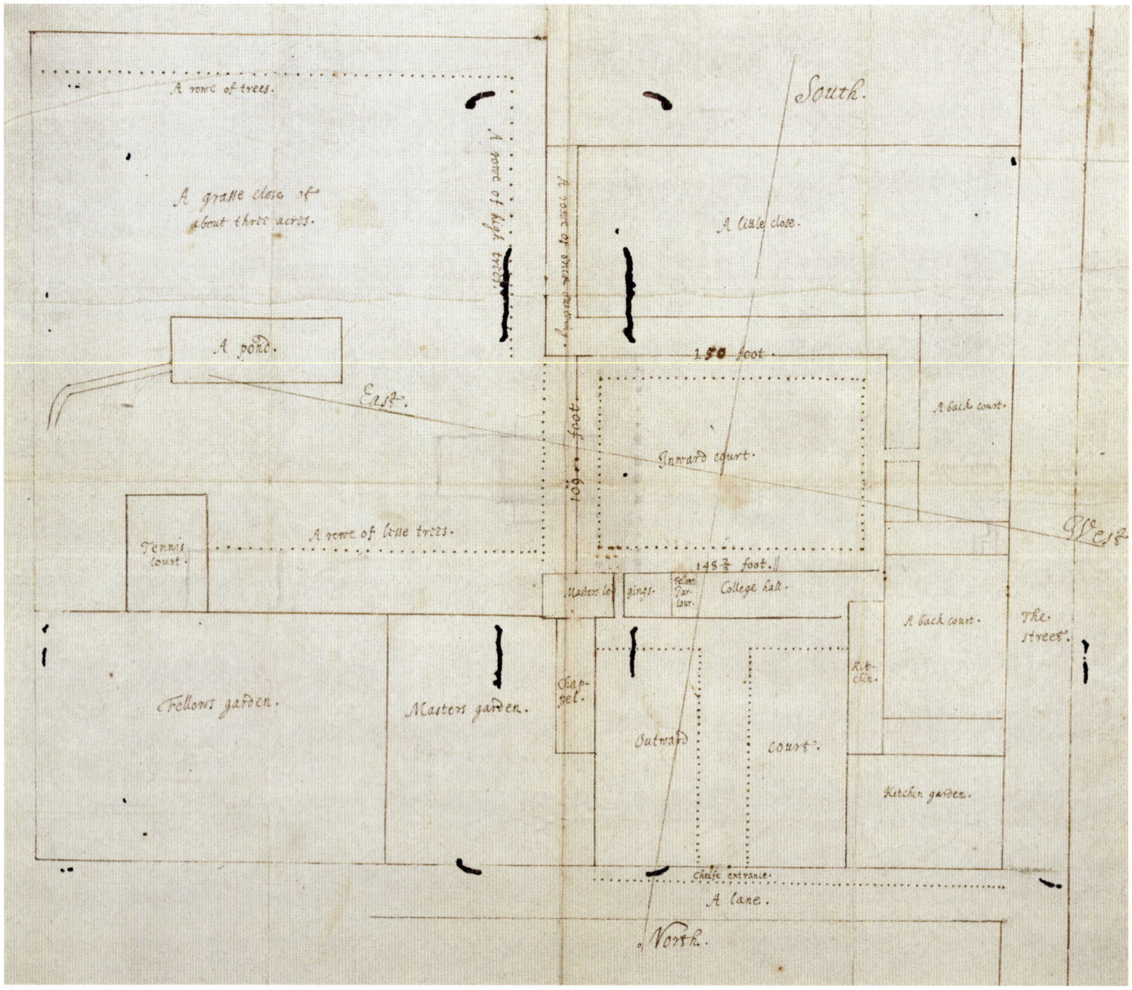

A survey of Emmanuel College, from around 1650, showing the extent of the buildings largely as laid out by Walter Mildmay with the addition of the mid-1630s' Old Court, also known as the 'Brick Building'.

Cambridge life could be a damp experience even then. The Dutch humanist and Greek scholar, Desiderius Erasmus, famously complained about the rain when teaching in Cambridge in the early 1500s – as a member of Queens' College – finding the weather quite as much of a disappointment as English beer.[17]

Part of Emmanuel's charm in the late sixteenth century, as today, were the ample grounds attached to the former Dominican house, which now became the private gardens of the College. From Hamond's 1592 map we can see that the Master's Garden was then more formally laid out than the adjoining Fellows' Garden. The map labels the park-like field as 'E[mmanuel] college walkes', suggesting a valued place of exercise and reflection.[18]

Mildmay's new College project seems to have been completed in a short time, to the approval of his peers in the University. Sir Thomas Legge, the Vice-Chancellor in 1587 and by no means a natural ally, wrote to Mildmay of his admiration for the 'Colledge, founded in your honour, and brought to suche perfection in so shorte a space ... a beautye and ornament is added to the Universitie'.[19]

The first Master of the College, Laurence Chaderton, appears to have occupied his own house built on the site of St Nicholas's Hostel, just across the road from the College to the north, with his wife and child as well as various undergraduates as lodgers. He may have perhaps used the austere Master's Lodge rooms in the College itself for teaching, for it was a requirement of the statutes that the Master should be resident, but perhaps the site of St Nicholas's Hostel was regarded as part of the College.[20]

William Dillingham, who knew Chaderton in his old age, was related to him by marriage and was also acquainted with his daughter, observed in his *Life of Chaderton*,

> *he thought it more convenient to leave the lodgings which the founder had designed for the master's use within the college walls, and to purchase another residence in the town. He accordingly secured the house which occupied the site of St Nicolas in the old University ... Chaderton soon made this house the home of varied learning, and from it came true heroes as from the Trojan horse. Hence came Richard, earl of Holland, chancellor; Finch, Lord Chief Justice and Lord Chancellor; Mildmay Fane, great-great-grandson of our founder.*[21]

By this he meant they lodged within Chaderton's household.

Chaderton was an active gardener and planter of trees who 'delighted himself in sampling and gathering plants': the rows of trees around the site visible in a mid-seventeenth-century survey (see opposite) can probably be attributed to him and set the tone for later replantings.[22] One former Emmanuel Fellow, Bishop William Bedell, wrote from Ireland, 'Remember me to Mr Chaderton ... ask if he will bestow on me two or three of his white mulberry trees – cutting off their heads – I would entreat you also to get me some grafts out of Emmanuel college gardens of the timely cherries'.[23]

Above all, Chaderton was a famously charismatic theologian, scholar and preacher, who became a dedicated but usually conforming Puritan. He studied at Christ's College Cambridge (where he became a Calvinist and was cut off by his Catholic father), and became a Fellow but gave up his Fellowship to marry. As Master of Emmanuel, he attracted the interest and confidence of the leading Puritan gentry and under his tenure the College grew to be, for a brief time in the early seventeenth century, the largest of the University, filled with well-connected youths destined for careers in Parliament or the Church. But, as Patrick Collinson notes, surprisingly the College:

> *sent rather fewer men into the ministry than other colleges of the same size, and recruited a larger number of gentleman commoners ... these prize pupils would become some of the great and good of*

early seventeenth-century England, whom Chaderton carefully cultivated, building up a benign country-wide alliance of magistracy and ministry.[24]

Mildmay's foundation clearly stimulated interest at court, and the seventeeth-century historian Thomas Fuller relayed a much-repeated Cambridge legend about him: 'Coming to court after he had founded his college, the queen told him, "Sir Walter I hear you have erected a puritan foundation." "No, Madam", saith he, "far be it from me to countenance any thing contrary to your established laws, but I have set an Acorn, which when it becomes an oak, God knows what will be the fruit thereof".'[25]

Mildmay had attempted to fix the character of the College with his founding statutes,[26] which spoke of creating, by allusion to the garden of Paradise,

some seed-plots of those most noble plants of Theology and right good learning, from the which such as had grown to maturity might be translated to all parts of the Church, that she being watered by their labours and increased by the gift of God, might come at last to a most flourishing and blessed estate.[27]

The statutes were indeed so tightly framed that it became impossible to combine senior membership of the College

The Elizabethan Chapel (now the Old Library), which formed a significant part of the 1580s' entrance court; gabled dormers lit chambers over the Chapel and were rebuilt in the nineteenth century. Note the increase in the number of gabled dormers.

[opposite] *Loggan's depiction of the Elizabethan Chapel range (by 1690 this had become the Library).*

with preferment in the Church at large.[28] This made traditional clerical career paths difficult: for instance, one could not be a College Fellow and serve as a chaplain to a great nobleman, the usual route to being noticed for significant appointments.

Mildmay's firm intention was that Fellows should not 'tarry' in College, but proceed to the degree of Doctor of Divinity, before leaving to become ministers and active preachers. This was to be as soon as the University statutes allowed, which seems to have been around ten years from taking the Fellowship, although they were expected to leave within a year of receiving their doctorates.[29] Undergraduates were also supposed to reside in College, wear sober clothes and only to go into town with permission. They should be 'always occupied, so far as they may be, either in the worship of God, or in the study of good learning'.[30]

But before we imagine this to be an entirely high-minded place, John Aubrey's *Brief Lives*, written in the late seventeenth century, gives one alternative glimpse of College life, and a hint of the conflict between the High Church and Puritan parties a century before:

> *The Puritan faction did begin to increase in those days, and especially at Emannuel … They preached up very strict keeping and observing the Lord's Day; made, upon the matter, damnation*

to breake it, and that 'twas lesse sin to kill a man ... Yet these hypocrites did bowle in a private green at their colledge every Sunday after sermon.[31]

Aubrey goes on to relate the story of how Lancelot Andrewes, the High-Church Master of Pembroke College from 1589 to 1605, entered the Emmanuel Fellows' Garden one Sabbath evening and 'discovered those zealous preachers with their gownes off, earnest at play' – with their bowls. Fellows' bowls are still kept in the Fellows' Garden today.

The early College Admonition Book also shows that it has never been easy to control the energies of young undergraduates, who would then have been 16 to 18 years old. Around 1586, one John Cook was formally admonished 'partly for disobedience to the Master and unreverend abusing of the Fellows by his stoute and Stubbourne behaviour & partly for bending a stone bowe and chargingg it with a pellet and intending it as he said only to fear Henry Baines who also he abused with uncharitable words'.[32] In 1587, the Master had to upbraid one Robert Thomson 'boath for abusing of his tounge in calling his fellow Rakell, also for abusing his hands in striking of him divers blows'. In 1590, Richard Challener was written up for 'disorderly behaviour in the Chapel but especially for talking and whistling in time of prayers to the great disturbance of the whole company'.[33]

The Chapel was intended as an especially important feature of Mildmay's College, but for its austerity rather than its riches. It was a new building constructed under Ralph Symons's guidance but, unlike Trinity College's Chapel built in the 1550s and 1560s partly from the stone of the dissolved Greyfriars' monastery, no attempt was made to echo late medieval glories. Aside from the arms of Elizabeth I in the north window, it was plain and functional, with a pulpit, hourglass, communion table and 'forms' (benches) for sitting. It was a preaching box, well lit by tall windows and large enough for the whole 'household' of the College; it is not quite clear how the altar or chancel was then disposed. The plain, open oak 'screen', which separated the Chapel from the entrance, revealed in the restoration in the 1930s, has a domestic character, and can be compared to the screen of the chapel at Hardwick Hall in Derbyshire.[34]

In fact, in 1603, the severity and nonconformity of Emmanuel's Chapel was heavily censured: 'First for a prognostication of disorder, whereas all the Chappels in the University are built with the Chancells Eastward according to the uniform order of all Christendom, the Chancell on t[ha]t College standeth north, and their kitchen eastwarde'.[35] It was also noted that all other colleges used the Prayer Book and followed the ordnance of the Church of England, whereas 'In Emmanuel College, they do followe a private course'. Members of the College had not worn surplices or academic hoods since the Chapel was 'first erected'. They did not fast, nor take communion kneeling: 'they receive that Holy Sacrament, sittinge upon Formes about the Communion Table, and doe pull the Loafe one from the other, after the Minister hath begon. And soe the Cupp, one drinking as it were to another, like good Fellows.'[36]

Chaderton was a radical and well-connected figure, but he skilfully stayed within the system. Attacked in the early 1600s for his lack of orthodoxy, he remained consistently pragmatic and conformed where necessary. He thought the surplice, sign of the cross and kneeling were 'things indifferent' so should neither be imposed, nor, he thought, need they be refused in all circumstances.

James I suggested to Sir Robert Cecil, then Chancellor of the University of Cambridge, that Chaderton could be removed 'if he continue obstinate', but Chaderton remained in office until retirement at around 86 years old, and then continued to live across the street, influencing College life up to his death at the grand age of about 103.[37] His retirement speech was noted by Dillingham as an emotional event 'like Paul saying farewell to the elders at Ephesus'.[38]

In the early years of the foundation, about 12 Fellows were responsible for the undergraduates. Benjamin Whichcote, one of the Cambridge Platonists, was a tutor at Emmanuel in the 1630s and recalled that 'employment with pupils took my time from me. I have not read many books.'[39] The College residential ranges consisted of sets of rooms, with three to four students sharing a combined living and sleeping room around the hearth, and screened-off private areas against the windows for study.

Surviving letters show undergraduates vying for the best rooms, ideally close to their tutors, and enjoying strong bonds of camaraderie and loyalty. There is also often evidence of the affection in which the College was held by graduates. For example, in a letter from the founder's great-grandson, 2nd Earl of Westmorland, to Master William Sancroft the Elder, he stressed his feeling of connection: 'Master, for so I must style you, as being a member of the college still, though discontinuance perhaps hath wiped my name out of the buttery tables or racked it quite out of the manciple's books'.[40] He hoped to find a lodging in the College on the occasion of a royal visit 'for I would be loth to lodge in any other than where I sucked my first milk'.

From the late 1620s, a number of Emmanuel's graduates and former Fellows took part in the Puritan migration, which was instrumental in shaping New England and in the evolution of modern America. In 1630, the *Arbella* was funded by a grandson of Laurence Chaderton and an Emmanuel man, Isaac

A map of the American colonies, published in Captain John Smith's A Description of New England *(1616).*

Johnson, who gave the ship the name of his wife, Lady Arbella (née Fiennes). The Johnsons both died in New England in 1630 but not before Isaac had named a settlement 'Boston' after the Lincolnshire hometown of preacher John Cotton, also, as it happens, an Emmanuel man.[41]

These Puritans went to help establish a purer version of the Christian Church than they believed even then possible in England and, as John Winthrop wrote: 'It will be a service to the Church of great consequence to carry the Gospel into those parts of the world ... & to raise a Bulwark against the kingdom of Ante Christ w[hi]ch the Jesuits labour to reare up in those parts'.[42]

The Emmanuel graduates who became part of the New England settlement were the unexpected oaks that grew from Mildmay's acorn. Samuel Morison, the historian of Harvard University, calculated that among the 129 Oxford and Cambridge men who arrived before 1650, 35 came from Emmanuel.[43] Many Emmanuel men occupied positions of great influence as preachers, theologians and statesmen, most notably John Cotton and Thomas Hooker. When they left England in 1633, one witness wrote: 'I saw the Lord departing

[following pages] *Old Court, completed in 1634 and first known as the Brick Building. It was restored in the eighteenth century and again in the twentieth century, but its original plan remains largely intact.*

THE
DOUGLAS
FINLAY
MUSEUM
OF COLLEGE
LIFE

Detail from Loggan's view of Emmanuel, showing Old Court from the west. The chimney stacks appear to have the character of classical columns; these chimneys and the gables have been removed.

from England when Mr. Hooker and Mr. Cotton were gone, and I saw the hearts of most of the godly set and bent that way, and I did think I should feel many miseries if I stayed behind'.[44]

Near Boston, a small settlement called Newtown was renamed Cambridge and became the home of a new college. In 1638, another Emmanuel graduate, John Harvard (b.1607), a London-born minister and 'godly gentleman', left this New England college half of his estate and his library. In gratitude, the overseers of the 'new' college resolved, 'that the college agreed upon formerly to be built at Cambridge shalbee [*sic*] called Harvard College'.[45] Thus one of the most influential academic institutions of the modern world has close and significant links to Emmanuel.

By 1642, Harvard College had a building, 'thought by some to bee too gorgeous for a wilderness'.[46] But back at Emmanuel, the nursery of so many of these New England pioneers, the College was growing beyond its old buildings. The first major alteration can be dated to 1634, when a range of new sets of rooms was added to the eastern end of the Founder's Range. This is Old Court (also once known as the 'Brick Building') running south from Front Court, comprising a single depth of rooms grouped around two staircases sited between chimneystacks, creating a mirror image set of rooms. Indeed, the plan followed the medieval pattern of shared living/bedrooms, with small studies off to the side, the latter well lit but without a hearth.[47]

Old Court is a three-storey building with an attic above, built in brick with stone arches to the east-facing entrances. Loggan's aerial view (published in 1690) shows fashionable shaped gables to the third-storey windows. The contract was with John Westley, bricklayer, and the carpenter was Henry Man.[48] The contract refers to the use of materials from the old tennis court (which was possibly part of the pre-foundation residential amenities of the Shirwood family home), as well as from the wall demolished to make way for the building.

This new building was completed by 1634. Fellow William Bennet described it 150 years later, in 1788, as in a 'tottering state, and only kept together by the strength of the chimneys'. This was probably an exaggeration but the gabled, brick dormers were presumably removed at this time. Bennet's view was that the original execution had been 'shamefully negligent',[49] but this has the ring of someone who wants a building replaced rather than repaired.

Since 1924, a Harvard scholar has been a regular feature of College life, housed in a dedicated set of rooms within Old Court, which was in fact completed just – but only just – before Harvard

An eighteenth-century view by an unknown artist, in ink and wash, of Old Court from the east, screened by an avenue of tall trees (possibly elms). Laurence Chaderton, the founding Master, had been an active planter of trees in the College grounds, which established the character of these tree-lined green spaces.

himself had graduated. Nonetheless, the repaired (and recently modernised) building is a tangible link to that early seventeenth-century College.

Old Court was being built during the time of Benjamin Whichcote (student and Fellow from 1626 to 1643), considered the father of a group of philosophers and theologians known as the Cambridge Platonists, 'by virtue of the fact that so many of them studied at Emmanuel College when he taught there'.[50] Less extreme than the Calvinists of the great migration, the group included Ralph Cudworth and Nathaniel Culverwell, and played an important part in the mid-century College and the intellectual life of the Restoration-era Church of England.

Whichcote's ideas are mostly known through collections of his writings posthumously published by his pupils. His tolerant, optimistic and rationalist approach was the hallmark of the group who held Plato, Plotinus and other ancient philosophers in high regard. Alongside their interest in these philosophies, they were also closely linked to new scientific thought. They maintained that the rational was not in opposition to the spiritual but rather a manifestation of divine power working in mankind. They also stressed that true religion was expressed in the love of God over the justice of God, and were the first generation of English philosophers to write their works in English only rather than in Latin.

The civil wars of the 1640s were problematic for Emmanuel, as for the University at large. Nevertheless, the Puritan character of Emmanuel protected it, as well as promoting the careers of some of its senior members.[51] Although in the town there

A 1682 portrait by Mary Beale (1633–1699) of Benjamin Whichcote (1609–1683), Emmanuel graduate and Fellow, and Commonwealth-era Master of King's College. He is regarded as the father of the Cambridge Platonists.

was no fighting in the streets, sieges or whole-scale destruction, it was for a time, in effect, under military occupation. Cambridge and its immediate area was already under the political influence of Oliver Cromwell and the 2nd Earl of Manchester. The town was originally largely for Parliament, with the colleges, on the whole, for the Crown. The unsettled times led to a collapse in undergraduate numbers and college income, and several heads of colleges were imprisoned for supporting Charles I. After the victory of Parliament, many college chapels were also subsequently stripped of suspect 'popish' images and practices.

The then Master of Emmanuel, Richard Holdsworth, was a Puritan by sympathy but also contributed to the king's cause and, in 1643, welcomed the king as he passed through Cambridge. Holdsworth managed to hold onto his Mastership and was elected Vice-Chancellor but was then deprived of it in 1644, summoned by Parliament and committed to the Tower of London, from which he was released the following year.[52]

The Commonwealth period also changed the status of Emmanuel: in 1650 the parliamentary committee for the reform of the universities ruled that the post-Reformation colleges (Emmanuel and Sidney Sussex) should become full members of the University and should share in the rotation of offices.[53] Emmanuel was, in fact, a particularly influential college at this time, for of the ten ejected Cambridge Masters, eight had been replaced by Emmanuel men.

Emmanuel's high-minded John Worthington replaced Richard Sterne as Master of Jesus College, although he was deeply embarrassed to profit from another's downfall. As the new Master of King's College, Whichcote also struggled to reconcile himself with the acceptance of a post taken from a respected colleague. Memorably, he gave half his annual dividend to his ejected predecessor and sought to reassure Worthington, telling him of Sterne, 'he cannot return if you give way'.[54]

William Sancroft the Younger, a Fellow of Emmanuel, observed: 'I had not thought they would have beheaded whole colleges at a blow; nay, whole universities and whole churches too'.[55] Sancroft eventually went into exile in Europe in the late 1650s, but returned at the Restoration and was appointed Master of Emmanuel. In his short tenure, from 1662 to 1665, he was to change substantially the tenor and destiny of Mildmay's great project, in architectural terms above all.

Mildmay's Chapel had been one of the few in Cambridge to escape rebuke under the Commonwealth. In 1640, the iconoclast appointed by Parliament, William Dowsing, had ordered the removal of carvings, images, stained glass and altar steps throughout Cambridge, but of Emmanuel's Chapel he merely noted that nothing 'needed to be mended'.[56] Just two decades later, William Sancroft concluded that there was much that needed to be mended to reform and revive Emmanuel, and the Chapel was at the heart of this.

SIR WALTER MILDMAY *c.*1523–1589

The founder of Emmanuel, Sir Walter Mildmay, was a distinguished public servant with great financial expertise.[57] The fifth son of Thomas Mildmay, a mercer of Chelmsford in Essex, he was a Fellow-Commoner at Christ's and admitted to Gray's Inn in 1546. First elected to Parliament in 1545, he married Mary, sister of Sir Francis Walsingham, before being knighted by Edward VI in 1547. By 1551 he had a country estate, Apethorpe, in Northamptonshire.

A confirmed Calvinist, he remained in conformity with the Church of England. Grace, Lady Mildmay, described her father-in-law as pious, humble, 'wise, eloquent and methodical in all his speeches', someone who would not 'allow men to speak ill of others'.[58] This careful, clever man rose steadily in public service, admired for his ability to resolve complex fiscal issues, such as compiling the inventory of Henry VIII's property.

His career slowed under Mary I as he overtly resisted the Catholic Restoration, but his skills meant he was quickly on the rise again. In the late 1550s, he became a knight of the shire for Northampton, a seat he retained until his death.[59] He worked closely with Lord Burghley, and was Chancellor of the Exchequer from 1559.[60] He was one of the key ministers involved in decisions surrounding Mary Queen of Scots and was among those who told her of her fate.[61]

Mildmay was keenly interested in education. In 1551, he and his brother petitioned to refound the grammar school at Chelmsford in the refectory of the former Black Friars' house there. In 1568, Mildmay endowed a Greek lecturer, preacher and scholars at his old college, Christ's Cambridge; then, in 1584, he founded Emmanuel College, once again using the buildings of a former Dominican house.

[left] *Detail of Sir Walter Mildmay, 1588, by an unknown artist.*

[opposite above] *Mrs Joyce Frankland, by an unknown artist.*

[opposite below] *Laurence Chaderton, from the conjectural portrait in the Chapel's Heaton, Butler & Bayne stained glass, 1884.*

DAME JOYCE FRANKLAND 1531–1587

Joyce (or Jocosa) Frankland was a formidable educational benefactor.[62] She was the daughter of Robert Trappes, a citizen and goldsmith of London, and his wife Joan, who was a benefactor of Lincoln College Oxford.

Joyce married twice: first Henry Saxey, a 'Merchant Venturer', then William Frankland of Rye House in Hertfordshire. With her first husband she had a son, William Saxey, a student of Gray's Inn who died at just 23. After the death of her second husband, she devoted her wealth to educational endowments.

Alexander Nowell, a somewhat opportunist Puritan-leaning Dean of St Paul's, recalled how on the death of her son, 'I, being of her acquaintance, having intelligence, did with all speed ride to her house near Hoddesdon to comfort her the best I could, and I found her crying, or rather howling, continually "Oh my son, my son!"'[63] Nowell concluded, 'God I think, put me in mind at the last to say "Comfort yourself good Mrs Frankland … if you would found certain fellowships and scholarships to be bestowed upon studious young men, who should be called Mrs Frankland's scholars, they would be in love towards you as dear children".'

Joyce thus founded a free school at Newport in Essex and added to scholarships endowed by her mother at Lincoln College Oxford. Her will, dated 20 February 1586, included Fellowships and scholarships at Emmanuel College as well as significant legacies to Brasenose College Oxford and to Gonville and Caius College Cambridge. Joyce Frankland's total educational benefactions during her lifetime and in her will were £4,840.

LAURENCE CHADERTON *c.*1536–1640

As the first Master, Laurence Chaderton was the clear choice of Walter Mildmay, who apparently told him: 'If you will be no Master, I will be no Founder'.[64] From his appointment in 1584, Chaderton stamped Emmanuel with its Puritan, 'godly' character as a seminary to train preachers for English pulpits while enhancing its surroundings with a programme of tree-planting.[65]

Chaderton was born into a Catholic gentry family in Oldham, Lancashire, where he pursued a sporting life. He turned Calvinist at Christ's College Cambridge and was a Fellow there from 1568 until 1577. He then resigned and married Cecily, daughter of wealthy London haberdasher Nicholas Culverwell, from a well-connected Puritan family. A renowned theologian, and scholar of Latin, Greek and Hebrew, Chaderton was chosen as one of the translators of the King James Bible. He was a popular preacher at St Clement's Church in Cambridge for 50 years. On one occasion, realising that he had preached for a full two hours, he offered to stop but the congregation cried out: 'For God's sake, sir, go on!'[66]

Although a Puritan, Chaderton, like Mildmay, remained within the law. Even as Master he seems to have lived in a house he built for his family across the street from the College, on the site of St Nicholas's Hostel, where he also accommodated young undergraduates from a network of Puritan gentry. In 1622, he resigned his 38-year Mastership in favour of John Preston, although he remained close by and outlived his successor, reaching the age of about 103 and becoming one of 'the treasured antiquities of Cambridge'. It was claimed that in his old age he could still read a Hebrew Bible without spectacles, and a book in Trinity College Library has clear and pertinent annotations made by Chaderton when he was 100. He died on 13 November 1640.[67]

3

Temple of Learning Renewed

A college is shaped by its 'society' and the individuals within it. Some individuals make more of a mark than others; one who did was William Sancroft, who played a key role in Restoration Emmanuel. He was the nephew of a former Master, and was Royalist in sympathy, High Church by inclination, and with a level of scholarship and administrative ability that elevated him to the post of Archbishop of Canterbury in 1677.

Back in 1651, he had resigned his Emmanuel Fellowship to escape ejection and spent the years 1657–60 travelling in the Netherlands, Geneva and Italy.[1] After the Restoration, he was snapped up as chaplain and then prebendary by John Cosin, Bishop of Durham and a former Master of Peterhouse (who also made him rector of Houghton-le-Spring). Sancroft was marked out for further preferment and made Master of Emmanuel in 1662. A royal mandate relieved him of the 'unusuall severity of your College Statutes', allowing him to retain his other offices, and the all-important income from these posts, for the Mastership of Emmanuel was not well endowed.[2]

After 1660, ten of the 16 Commonwealth-era heads of houses were ejected, five being originally Emmanuel men (eight had become heads during the Commonwealth). Sancroft remained on friendly terms with William Dillingham, who was ejected in 1662 for failing to accept the Restoration settlement. They had shared rooms as undergraduates and Dillingham wrote in a friendly spirit offering his academic robes 'which you may please freely to make use of'.[3]

In 1662, Sancroft arrived at the College he had loved as an undergraduate to find himself something of a stranger, 'my acquaintance being wholly worne out'. He observed that he had 'come into a new college, quite another thing from what I, and much more from what you, left it'.[4] Emmanuel had also undoubtedly lost much of the high-minded radical character that had made it such a honeypot for sons of the 'great and good', but its intellectual confidence had also declined.[5] Sancroft wrote to his former tutor 'I find not that old genius and spirit of learning

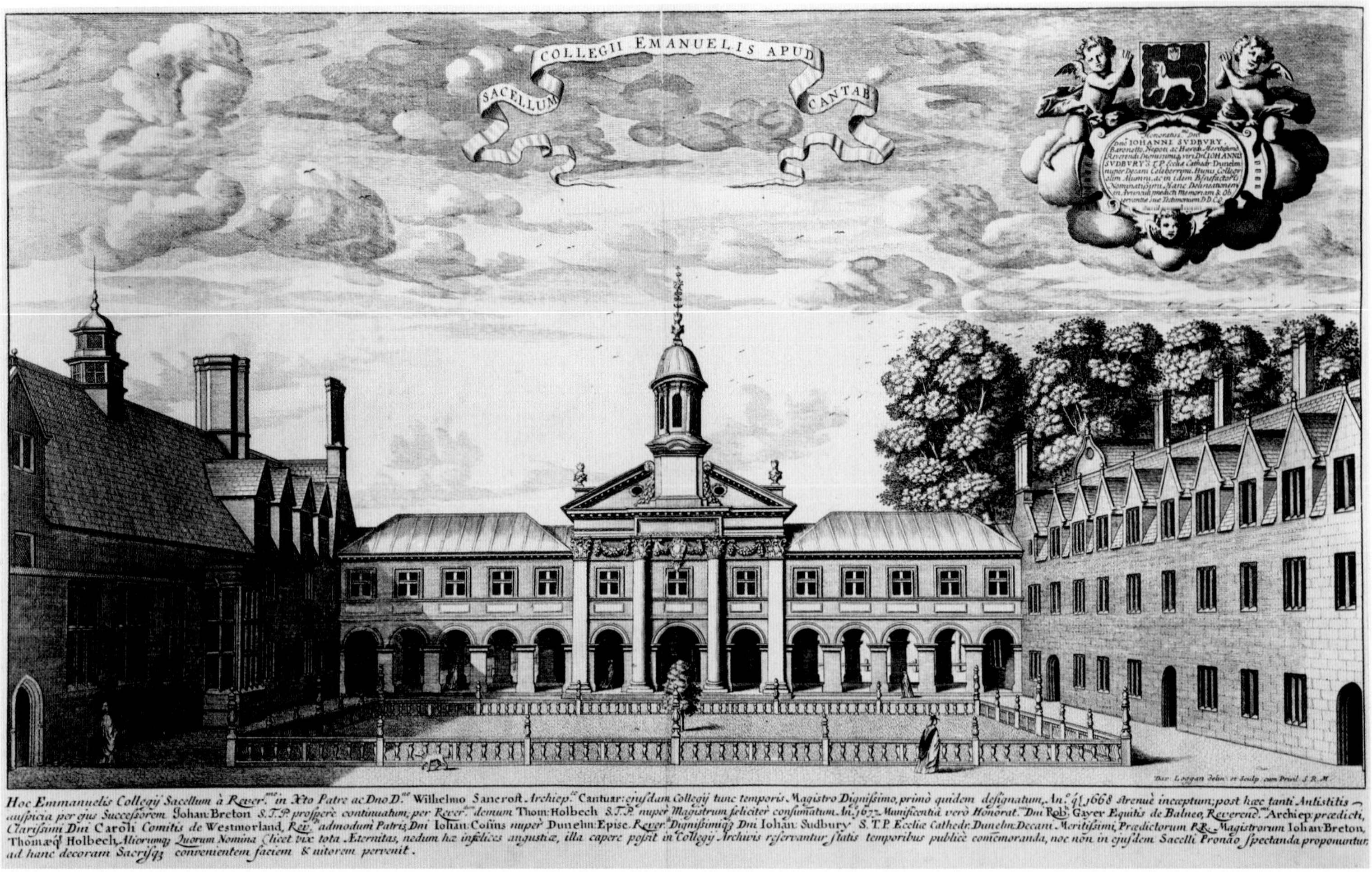

[previous pages] *The College revived: Wren designed this new eastern range by 1665, with a Cloister opening into what is now Front Court. The bold temple-front treatment of the centre gives a strong visual focus (and can be loosely compared to the south front of Wren's first prestigious building, the Sheldonian Theatre, in Oxford). The first-floor Gallery runs the full length of the range, and the temple-front marks the dimension of the Chapel, which runs eastwards behind the Gallery.*

generally in the college that made it once so deservedly famous' and that it would be hard to build the College's reputation 'till the fellowships and scholarships be made competent … [and] till the body of our statutes be changed'.[6]

In the same letter, Sancroft outlined his ambition to claim the library of former Emmanuel Master, Richard Holdsworth, who had left his books to the College provided a fit room was found for them:

> *For the performance whereof, & also for the removing of that great Mark of Singularity, wh[ic]h all the World so talks of, in the unusual prospect & Dress of the Chapel (different from that of other Colledges), I have it in designe to make both a new Library and Chapell too: & as to the manner of the contriving of both I would gladly receive yo[u]r particular Opinion'.*[7]

Sancroft was a perceptive patron of architecture who owned a copy of Henry Wotton's *The Elements of Architecture* (1624) and was involved in numerous construction projects throughout his career. In fact, he built or restored wherever he went, including the renovation of the Deanery House at York (where he was

[above] *Detail showing Loggan's view of the Chapel, with the more formally railed-in court. The Elizabethan Hall and Founder's Range are shown largely unchanged in character.*

[opposite] *A map of Cambridge dating from 1634, which shows the College to the extreme right (just above the arms of Viscount Camden) before the addition of the Chapel designed by Wren.*

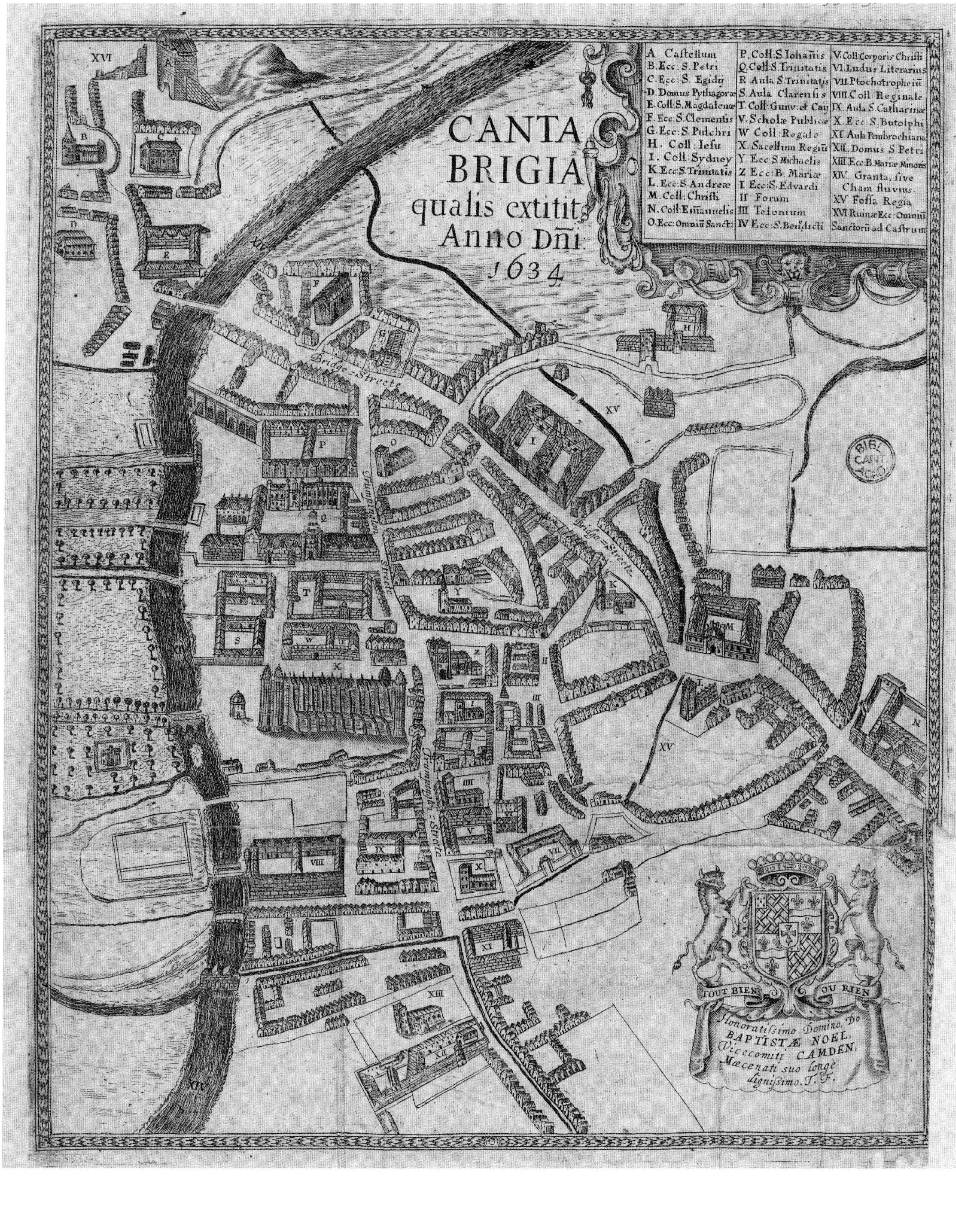

CANTA
BRIGIA
qualis extitit
Anno Dñi
1634
A Castellum
B. Ecc: S. Petri
C. Ecc: S. Egidij
D. Domus Pythagoræ
E. Coll: S. Magdalenæ
F. Ecc: S. Clementis
G. Ecc: S. Pulchri
H. Coll: Iesu
I. Coll: Sydney
K. Ecc: S. Trinitatis
L. Ecc: S. Andreæ
M. Coll: Christi
N. Coll: Emanuelis
O. Ecc: Omniũ Sanct:
P. Coll: S. Iohãnis
Q. Coll: S. Trinitatis
R Aula S. Trinitatis
S. Aula Clarensis
T. Coll: Gunv: et Caij
V. Scholæ Publicæ
W Coll: Regale
X. Sacellum Regiũ
Y. Ecc: S. Michaelis
Z Ecc: B. Mariæ
I Ecc: S. Edvardi
II Forum
III Telonium
IV Ecc: S. Benedicti
V. Coll: Corporis Christi
VI. Ludus Literarius
VII. Ptochotropheiũ
VIII. Coll: Reginale
IX. Aula S. Catharinæ
X. Ecc: S. Butolphi
XI. Aula Pembrochiana
XII. Domus S. Petri
XIII. Ecc: B. Mariæ Minoris
XIV. Granta, sive Cham fluvius.
XV Fossa Regia
XVI. Ruinæ Ecc: Omniũ Sanctorũ ad Castrum
Bridge-Streete
Trumpington Streete
TOUT BIEN OU RIEN
Honoratissimo Domino, Do
BAPTISTÆ NOEL,
Vicecomiti CAMDEN,
Mæcenati suo longè
dignissimo. T. F.

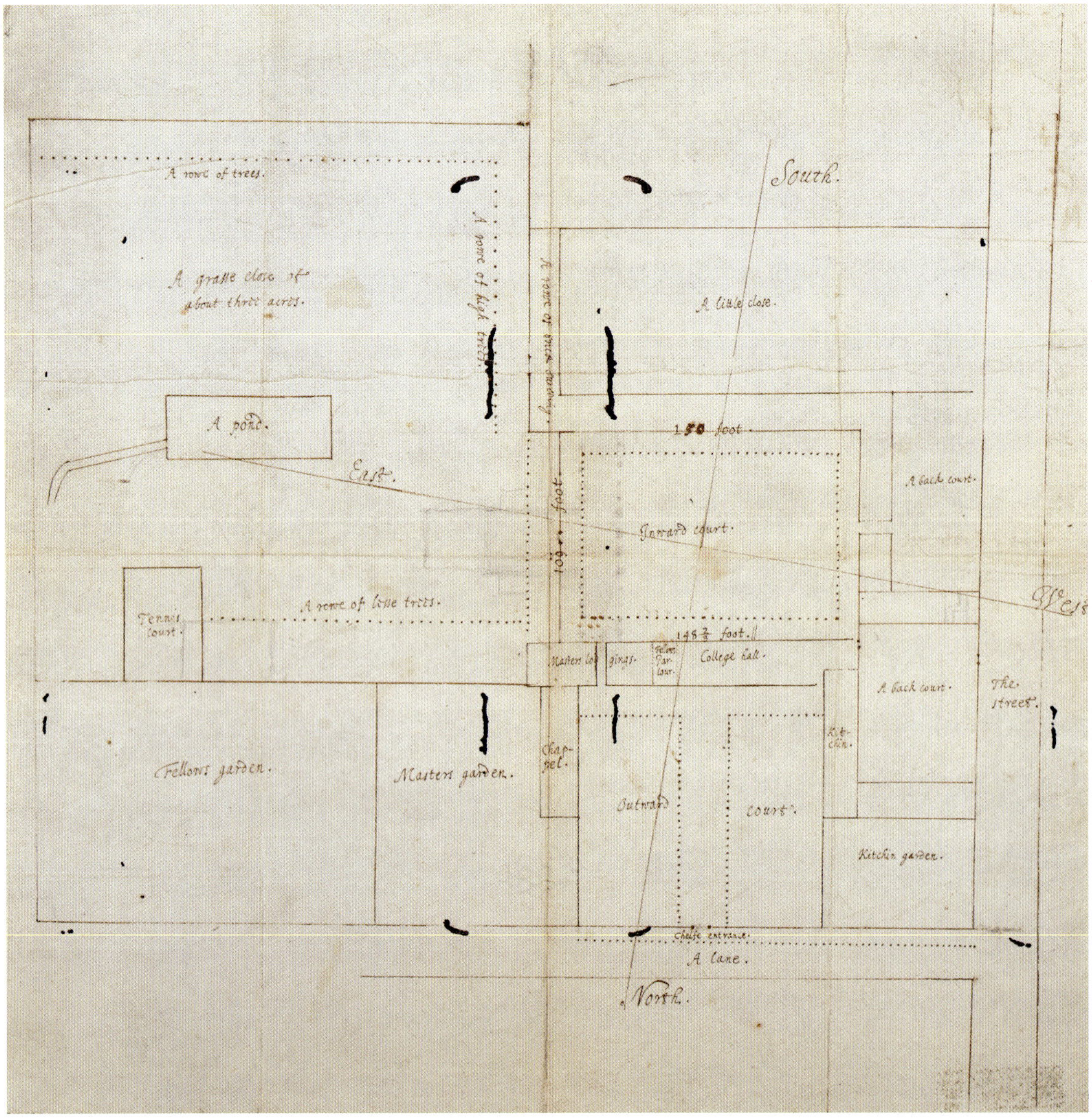

A survey of the College from around 1650, which shows the disposition of the College buildings before the addition by Wren. The link between the southern and northern ranges reads only as a simple wall, whereas in Hamond's 1592 map there is the suggestion of an arcade. It shows how confined the Master's Lodge was and the 'rows' of trees.

appointed Dean in January 1664) and then at St Paul's (where he was appointed Dean in November 1664), where a new Deanery House was built for him, designed by Christopher Wren's assistant, Edward Woodroofe.[8] Sancroft owned numerous architectural treatises, some of which were acquired on his travels on the Continent in the late 1650s. Among the books he later gave to Emmanuel was Roland Freart's *Parallele de L'architecture antique et de la Modern* (1650) and Pierre Le Muet's *Manière de bien bastir pour toutes sortes de personnes* (1647).[9] In 1677 he became Archbishop of Canterbury and continued the restoration of Lambeth Palace begun by Archbishops Juxon and Sheldon; a new range he added in the 1680s was, however, entirely demolished and replaced in the 1820s.[10]

At Emmanuel, as this 1662 letter shows, from the start Sancroft envisaged new buildings as a route to restoring the College's scholarly reputation. He was especially determined to create a Chapel for the sake both of the College and the revived Anglican Church. For this Sancroft turned to a rising star with impeccable Anglican connections, the Oxford astronomer and architect Wren, then at work on the Sheldonian Theatre in Oxford. Wren was the son of a canon of Windsor and a nephew of Matthew Wren, the Laudian Bishop of Ely (the scourge of the Puritans, Bishop Wren had been imprisoned in the Tower under the Commonwealth).[11] Sir Walter Mildmay's original Chapel was self-consciously plain, formally unconsecrated and traditionally understood to have been deliberately sited to run north–south, and not oriented towards the east.

As a protégé of John Cosin, the former Master of Peterhouse, Sancroft was very aware of the distinctive Peterhouse Chapel with its adjoining rooms over open arcades, an ambitious project of Matthew Wren of 1628–1633, and completed by Cosin. This arrangement provided one point of visual reference for the new Chapel at Emmanuel.[12] Emmanuel's design may also have echoed the role of the arcaded link buildings either side of the Chapel at Peterhouse, one thought to provide a route from the Master's Lodge to a projecting balcony-cum-gallery in the Chapel, suitable for the processional approach of a visiting king who could use it in the manner of a private pew (at Emmanuel the organ was not installed in this balcony until the 1680s, so it may have also served as a pew for the Master's family).[13]

The other local model was Christopher Wren's own early post-Restoration commission from his bishop uncle to design and build a new Chapel for Pembroke College – 1663–65 – the classical west elevation of which was inspired by a plate from Sebastiano Serlio's *Architettura*, first published in English in 1611.[14] That Chapel, an affirmation of the Restoration, is an important landmark in Cambridge; it is its earliest significant classical building and thought to be Wren's first completed building – even if it was the result of a close collaboration with Edward Pearce, the sculptor.[15] Its western end is crowned with a lantern, which helps give the building distinction and visual focus, as at Emmanuel. As A.V. Grimstone has illustrated, the team of craftsmen working on Emmanuel was very similar to that of Pembroke.[16]

At Emmanuel, this frontispiece to the arcaded Cloister and Gallery, which announces the Chapel, also has a distinct echo of the south front of the Sheldonian Theatre in Oxford, Wren's most prestigious early public commission – built 1664–69 – with its central pediment, and its division into an implied ground-floor arcade and low first-floor windows.[17] This front of the

Portrait of Sir Christopher Wren (1632–1723), 1711, by Godfrey Kneller (1646–1723), shown with his designs for St Paul's Cathedral.

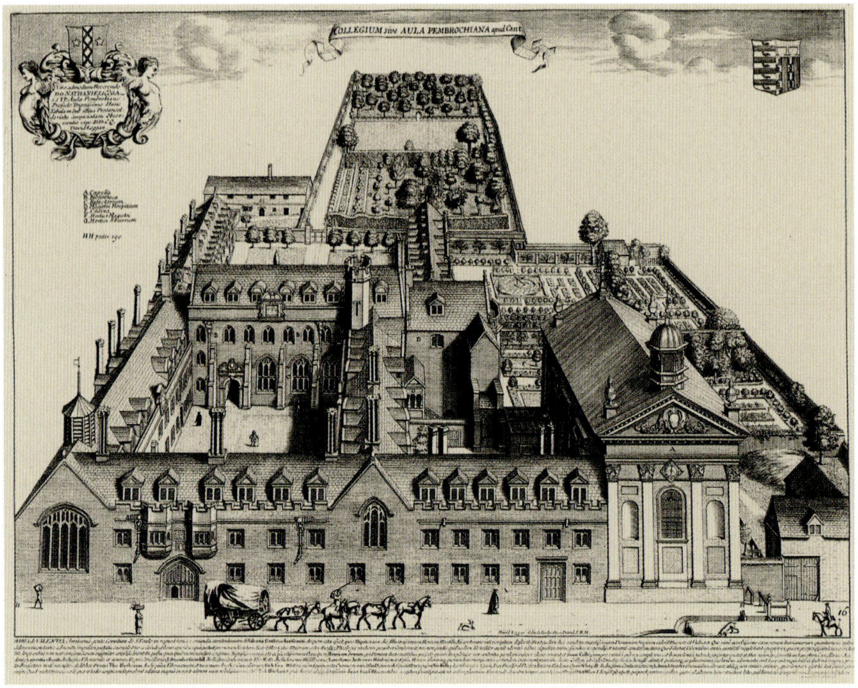

Loggan's view of the 1628–33 Chapel at Peterhouse built for Matthew Wren, seen from the inner court; the Chapel was conceived as an independent east-oriented structure (facing the street), flanked by an open arcade with rooms over. This could well have been a useful model for Christopher Wren's work at Emmanuel.

Loggan's view of Pembroke shows the Chapel, begun in 1663 and consecrated in 1665, which was Christopher Wren's earliest work in Cambridge (and on which he collaborated with the craftsman Edward Pearce) with a classical temple-front (inspired by a plate in Sebastiano Serlio's Architettura*). The Chapel was commissioned by Bishop Matthew Wren. It had a transformative effect on the character of the College and signalled the arrival of classical architecture in Cambridge. Published in 1690, this view is thought to date to 1681–82.*

Loggan's view of the south front of the Sheldonian Theatre in Oxford, designed by Christopher Wren for Gilbert Sheldon, Wren's first prestigious commission. Built in 1664–69, it shares some key motifs with Emmanuel and was in part inspired by Palladio's reconstruction of the Temple of Peace.

The Gallery, which runs above the Cloister and from which the Chapel gallery can be entered. Although this became a Long Gallery or Picture Gallery attached to the Master's Lodge by the time it was fitted out, it seems possible that it might have been first intended as a library space, as it is known that William Sancroft wanted to provide a more dignified and useful library for the College from his appointment as Master in 1662.

Sheldonian seems to have been in part modelled on Palladio's reconstruction of the Temple of Peace (the Basilica of Maxentius) as illustrated in *I Quattro Libri* (1570).[18] The more decorative quality of the central emphasis and surface carving at Emmanuel is also seen as evidence of the influence of Wren's 1665 visit to Paris.[19] Emmanuel's domed lantern has a distinctive quality that draws the eye up, and the two central engaged columns of the centrepiece bring the whole composition forward.

Pembroke and Emmanuel Chapels are both of significance as evidence of Wren's earliest efforts in architecture – along with Oxford's Sheldonian Theatre. There is a touch of experimentation here, and Kerry Downes has noted how 'the Chapel range at Emmanuel is one of those buildings which seem jewel-like or model-like because their vocabulary is larger in scale than their actual dimensions'.[20]

It is at least possible that the combined elements of the new building at Emmanuel (the Gallery over the arcade and the Chapel) began as that ambition of which Sancroft had spoken in 1662, of providing both a 'new Library and Chapell too'. Most sixteenth- and seventeenth-century libraries in Cambridge were on the first floor to benefit from increased light and protection against damp, and the scale of the Gallery was not so very different from the intimate 1580s' library of Trinity Hall. The 1670s library at Lincoln Cathedral, a new building over an arcade (over the ruins of the monastic cloister), also followed this pattern and Wren was also involved in that project.[21] While on a much larger scale, Wren's great library for Trinity College Cambridge – built 1676–84 – was also raised over an open colonnade.[22]

Sancroft resigned the Mastership in May 1665 to meet the challenges of his post as Dean of St Paul's (to which he was appointed in late 1664). A protracted legal case ending in 1664 also meant that the Holdsworth library went to the University, with duplicates and a sum of money arriving at Emmanuel in 1671. So by the time Wren provided his model and design, any early ambition for an associated new library (if it existed) may well have faded.[23]

Thus it can only be a matter of speculation that the Emmanuel Gallery may have originally been conceived of as a library. By the 1680s, the room is certainly listed in accounts as 'The Master's Gallery' with the acquisition of '39 turky work Chairs, 2 Spanish Tables, and 2 wrought carpets', and the room remained so-named until the 1930s.[24] The Gallery considerably amplified the accommodation of the Master's Lodge and was hung with portraits.

The original colour scheme of the interior of the Gallery is not known. Payments to painter John Wiseman for decoration in the 1670s make reference to 'whiting'; in the 1740s it was painted 'three times over finished with bright olive colour in oil'.[25] The nineteenth-century graining was replaced by an apple-green-based scheme in the mid-1980s, and with a more vivid blue-green proposed by the then Master, Lord St John of Fawsley, in the 1990s.

Sancroft continued to take the greatest interest in the planning of the Chapel and Gallery and was himself the major donor to the project and fundraiser, even after he had resigned as Master.[26] It is interesting to note that his list of benefactors for the Chapel was headed by notable royalist, collector and patron of art, Sir Robert Gayer, whom Sancroft had accompanied on a tour of the Rhineland, Geneva and Italy in the 1650s. Gayer had funded Sancroft's travels then, and gave £1,040 in all to the Chapel at Emmanuel.[27] In the 1680s Gayer also presented the altar and furnishings (including carving by Grinling Gibbons) to Wren's St James's, Piccadilly.[28]

Wren's single surviving design for the Emmanuel Chapel, now at All Soul's Oxford (see page 64), shows a gallery over a

[opposite] *Wren's original design for the Chapel range, probably of 1665 or 1666. It is unusual among Wren's designs in having the careful and full colour-wash treatment, indicating the wings were originally to be of brick, the roofs slate and perhaps the cupola timber covered in lead. There were later various modifications, including the redesign of the central window of the first floor and the variation of the first-floor window treatment generally. The central arch on the ground floor is shown as it was built; it was subsequently widened.*

Portrait of John Breton, the Master who began the actual building of the Chapel and Cloister designed by Wren, and who in 1668 travelled to Northamptonshire to sign the contract for the stone. He is depicted with the Chapel (as built with the widened central archway) but it had not been completed internally by the time he died in 1676.

The art of building: the fall of the light within Wren's Cloister is one of the most memorable architectural sensations of the College.

cloister in brick with stone dressings and a temple-like frontispiece.[29] It varies from the Chapel as built by the presence of two chimneys on the eastern (Paddock) side, and in certain aspects of detail, for instance, the size of the windows and the more attenuated proportion of the lantern's turret (which may have been altered to read more happily with the then existing lantern of the Hall, removed in the 1760s). The red-brick-and-stone combination of the drawing has been compared to the arcades of the much-admired early seventeenth-century Place Royale (now Place des Vosges) in Paris.[30]

The colour-wash treatment of this design (relatively rare among Wren's drawings) also suggests that the lantern may have originally been conceived as timber and covered in lead, while in its final form it is in stone with a lead-covered cupola. The Gallery arcade was called the 'cloyster' from as early as 1668, when the accounts are headed 'the particulars of the expenses of the chappell, cloysters, gallery', although there is also one reference to the 'portico gallery'.[31]

Sancroft's successor, John Breton, was also High Church and, like Sancroft, nominated by royal mandate. Senior Fellow Robert Alefounder observed of the method of his appointment in a letter to Sancroft: 'This I thinke was the onely way to preserve unity among us, and to satisfy owr selves and all other our friends abroad: it is easier to obey then to chuse'.[32] Breton took up the Chapel project with enthusiasm, although communication with Wren still seems to have been mostly conducted through Sancroft.

In 1667, the Master and Fellows were in receipt of the wooden model of Wren's design. Master Breton wrote to Sancroft:

> *We are much pleased with the model of our chappel: I yet meet with nothing to be added to your observations concerning it; only we wish it could be raised to a greater height, and if we have not an East window (concerning which we are of my Lord of Duresme's [Bishop of Durham's] opinion) it is thought it will be necessary that the side windows be enlarged.*[33]

IN MEMORIAM

The original 1670s' side staircase leading up to the Gallery, seen through a door on the north side of the Ante-Chapel.

Wren does not appear to have followed these suggestions, nor is it clear who was responsible for the resulting choice of scale and proportion, which were to be so significant for the future character of the College; inside the Chapel, they also enforced a degree of sacramental intimacy on those within.

In January 1668, Breton wrote to Sancroft, 'we prepare for the foundation of our Chappell, and much desire Dr. Wren's advice on the place'. Breton wrote again in February, 'I am in some readiness to begin, I will stay many days rather then want his advice upon the place. His presence will be a great reputation (besides other advantages) to the whole work. Give me leave to ask earnestly of you to use your power with him.'[34]

It was Breton who signed the contract for the building with Simon Wise of Deene, and Nicholas Ashby of Ketton supplied the stone. The old wall was demolished, the site pumped clear of water after 'the great rain made us some unexpected troubles which we shall soon overcome by pumping and fayr wether',[35] and timber delivered, including 40 trees from Apethorpe, the home of Charles Fane, 3rd Earl of Westmorland, a descendant of Sir Walter Mildmay. Wren's only recorded visit was in October 1668, which may have been when the decision was taken to build (or even possibly rebuild) the lantern in stone.[36]

The Chapel – which in Christopher Wren Jr's *Parentalia* (1750) is coupled with Trinity's great library and described as 'elegant' – was mostly structurally complete by 1672, although 1673 was chosen for the date stone.[37] John Grove II of St James's, London, was paid for plastering the ceiling and the walls in 1672, the year the bell was cast by Whitechapel founder Anthony Bartlet.[38] Further donations after the appointment of Master Thomas Holbech in 1675, an early supporter of the project, saw a determined move to complete everything after a slowdown in 1673–74.

Edward Pearce and John Oliver, who often worked with Wren, provided designs for the interior wainscot and seating, and Cornelius Austin the Elder was paid for executing these designs.[39] John Florry, a London mason, was paid for the marble flooring. The decision was taken to widen the central arch of the 'cloister', which led to the entrance to the Chapel, as it was presumably found too small for processional entry, and mason Robert Grumbold was paid for this. Sancroft was not able to attend the consecration on Michaelmas Day 1677 because of ill health, but Holbech wrote to tell of him of the consecration 'of our (or rather your) Chappell'.[40]

It seems Sancroft's views about converting the old Chapel into a new Library were sought only after the consecration of the Chapel, for Dillingham wrote to Sancroft as if this was a wholly novel idea in 1678.[41] The floor of the old Chapel was at

[left] *The Chapel, looking west, with the gallery into which the organ was fitted in 1686. The stalls and panelling were designed by Edward Pearce and John Oliver, and executed by the Cambridge joiner Cornelius Austin. The magnificent ceiling was by John Grove of London. The Chapel cost £3,972, which was covered by donations.*

[opposite] *The east orientation of the altar was an important motive for building the new Chapel; when consecrated in 1677 there was only an altar and hangings and in 1687 a fine carved oak reredos was added. The painting of* The Return of the Prodigal Son *by Giacomo Amigoni (1682–1752) was installed in 1734, and the glass chandelier in 1732. The Chapel was reordered by Arthur Blomfield in 1883–84 to reflect liturgical revival, and the arrangement of the east end altered to reflect this. In 2004 the Chapel was returned to its 1680s' character, with its eighteenth-century elements retained.*

least raised to avoid damp for its role as the Library. Cornelius Austin refitted the older wainscot and provided bookcases and other furniture.[42] The mason Grumbold created a window at the north end of the room: daylight was essential to the good operation of a library. In 1705–7 further bookcases (by John Austin) were introduced under the windows and between Cornelius Austin's original cases to accommodate the large collection of books Sancroft had given to the College before his death in 1693, described by the then Master in his letter of thanks as 'the most valuable treasure of your Grace's books'.[43]

When one of his (former) chaplains visited Sancroft shortly before his death, Sancroft discussed the way the books might be incorporated in Emmanuel's Library and suggested new cases could be placed below the windows, but 'he still tooke Time to consider, whether it should be so, or a new Fabric; and I have heard nothing further since this time'.[44] This rather suggests that Sancroft was still musing on a more suitable new library building for the College, to equal the glories of the Chapel, even at this late date.

Sancroft had also continued to take an interest in the fitting out of his Chapel: he had funded the wainscot himself.[45] In 1677, it had been furnished with a communion table and rails and the wall behind hung with purple and Carnation coloured satin as 'the clothe behind the altar', with the communion table covered in a velvet cloth. In the early 1680s an organ was added after a gift from Fellow-Commoner Burch Hothershall.[46] Sancroft clearly felt the hangings much too modest and gave money for the handsome pedimented reredos with its Corinthian columns of fine quality, which was erected in 1687 along with the carved rail enclosure.[47] (The altar painting arrived later, in the 1730s.)

All this stately magnificence was completed shortly before political events saw Sancroft driven from office, making the new Chapel at Emmanuel one of his greatest personal memorials (even given his famous association with Wren's St Paul's, where Sancroft played a key role in promoting the new design).[48] The first crisis was his stand against James II's order in council for the Declaration of Indulgence (which lifted the religious penal laws and introduced greater tolerance for non-Anglican Christian denominations) without the approval of Parliament. Sancroft and six leading bishops opposed this and were arrested, committed to the Tower and tried for sedition. They were acquitted and released.

[right] *The 1580s' Chapel converted to a Library in the 1680s, with some late nineteenth-century modifications, photographed in 1904.*

From a photograph by] [*J. Palmer Clarke, Cambridge*

[opposite] *The 'dais' end of the Hall, the panelling of which dates from the last decade of the seventeenth century, funded by Sir William Temple and others, with richly carved Corinthian pilasters and a portrait of Emmanuel's founder, Sir Walter Mildmay.*

Loggan's bird's-eye view of the whole College seen from the west, published in 1690. It gives a strong impression of the significant visual impact of the new classical element introduced into the Elizabethan and medieval courts, which seems to demand the reorienting of the College on the east–west axis that followed a century later. The extensive enclosed field within the College is part-framed by rows of tall trees; the Master's Garden and Fellows' Garden are also densely planted, as is the southern court (now known as Chapman's Garden).

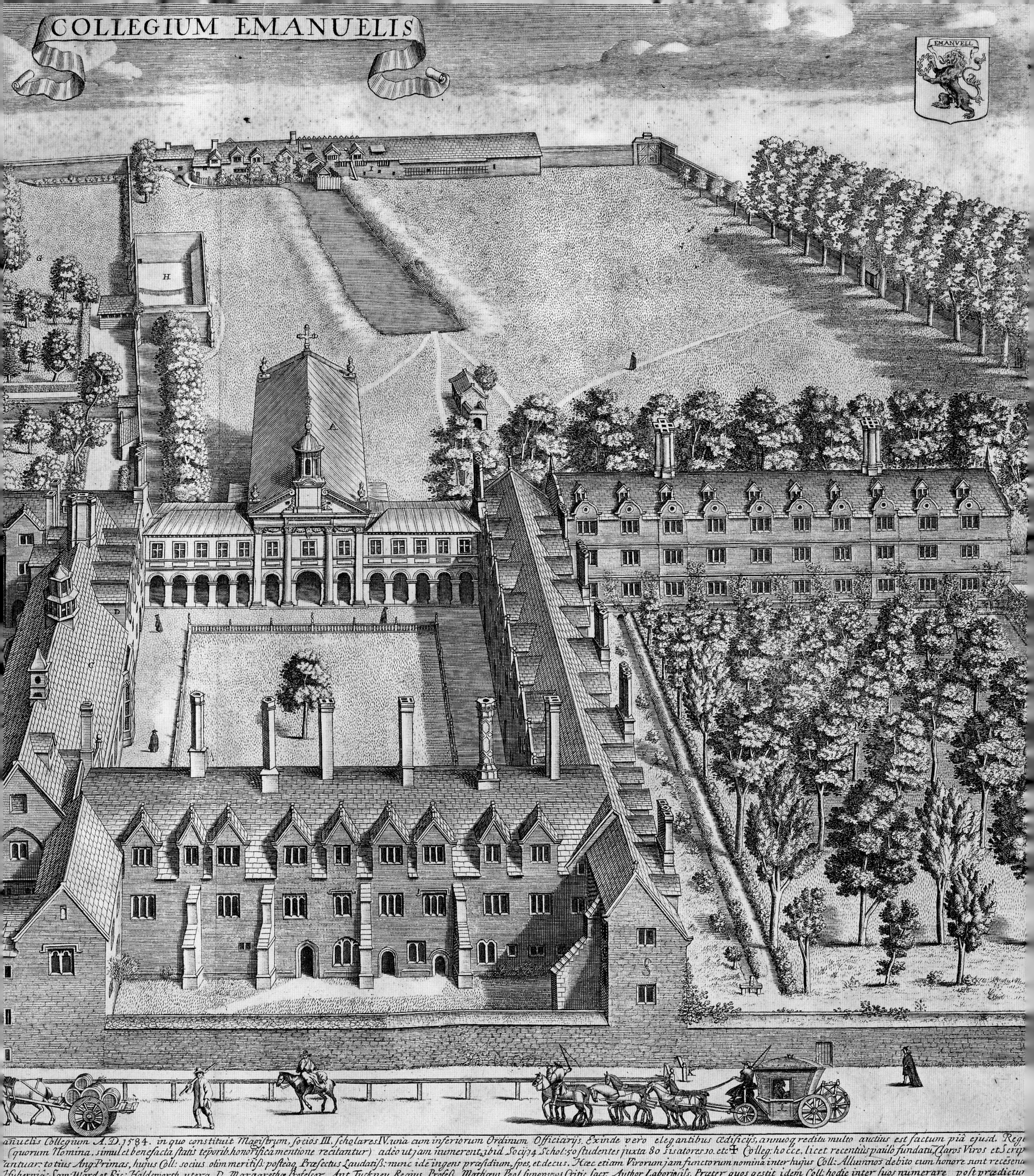

añuelis Collegium A.D.1584. in quo constituit Magistrum, socios III. scholares IV. unà cum inferiorum Ordinum Officiarijs. Exinde verò elegantibus ædificijs, annuoq reditu multo auctius est factum piâ ejusd. Reg
(quorum Nomina, simul et benefacta statis teporib. honorificâ mentione recitantur) adeò ut jam numerent, ibid Socij 14 Schol: 50 studentes juxta 80 sisatores 10. etc ✠ Colleg: ho cce, licet recentiùs paulò fundatũ, Claros Viros et Scrip
antuar: totius Ang. Primas, hujus Coll: socius olim meritiss: posteàq Præfectus Laudatiss: nunc idẽ ingens præsidium, spes, et decus. Hæc etiam Virorum jam functorum nomina inter hujus Coll: Allumnos debito cum honore sunt recẽsena
Hyberniæ; Sam: Ward et Ric: Holdsworth uterq, D. Margarethæ Professor Ant. Tuckney Regius Profess. Mathæus Pool synopsews Critic sacr: Author Laboriosiss. Prætrr quos gestit idem Coll: hodie inter suos numerare post prædictu
baco Reg. Illiq secudũ D. Tho. Iones Milit Cap. Iust. de com Banco, Viros Consultiss omniq laude majores Asserit quoq sibi D: Wilhel. Temple varijs pro Reg Majestate CAROLI·II. legationib. apud exteros functũ Edm: Castle S.T.P. hodiernum lingu: Arab
allis Geom. Profess: (nunc) apud Oxon: Item D. Wilhel Croon M.D. apud Londin. cum alijs quamplurimis, quorum nomina jamnunc in honore sunt, et apud posteros erunt in perpetuum. {Impræsentiarum Iohañ: Balderston S. T. P. et Canonicus Petroburg: est hujus Collegij Magister.

32

An anonymous oil on board depiction of the College based on Loggan's view and which hangs in the College today. It shows the comfortable well-planted setting of the College buildings, although the position of the horizon at the top of the picture, suggesting the complete isolation of the College, gives a bizarre impression.

For a time this made Sancroft a popular hero, but the event helped spark the Glorious Revolution: the very day they were acquitted, senior statesmen sent their invitation to William and Mary to take the Crown of England. This was a fresh twist, leading to a period of turmoil for establishment churchmen, with Sancroft at their head. He could remember the civil wars and had experienced exile, but appeared frozen into inaction and unable to compromise. Unwilling to crown or swear an oath to the new monarchs, Sancroft's hesitant but principled stand led to the end of his career.

The Emmanuel Master who completed the Chapel, Thomas Holbech, also founded one of the earliest known University lecture courses in ecclesiastical history. Lectures were delivered in Latin and the lecturer was asked to pay special attention to the ecclesiastical history of the British Isles and to those matters 'as still remain controversial'.[49] What more fitting place to give this lecture than a newly constituted Chapel, which could be seen as a symbol of attempts to draw together the spirit of the established church after decades of conflict and defeats?

Holbech's successor as Master of Emmanuel was John Balderston, who when elected as Vice-Chancellor in 1687 had to stand up to James II. A 'man of much spirit', he said that 'neither religion nor the rights of the body should suffer by his means'.[50]

But the same problems rumbled on. William Law, a convinced Jacobite, was ejected from his Emmanuel Fellowship as a non-juror in 1716, a continuation of the same issues of conscience that had unseated Sancroft. Law was tutor to the classical historian Edward Gibbon, and is best known for *A Serious Call to the Devout and Holy Life* (1729), admired by Samuel Johnson and cited as an inspiration by John and Charles Wesley, the founders of Methodism.[51]

Towards the end of the seventeenth century, David Loggan engraved his famous bird's-eye view of Emmanuel, part of the *Cantabrigia Illustrata* set of views of all the colleges made in the 1680s, and published in 1690.[52] This gives us a very clear picture of the physical character of the College at this date. Loggan was born in Gdańsk, Poland, but moved to England and worked as an engraver to the University of Oxford and then Cambridge. His general view of Emmanuel (from the west) is a detailed and precise study, which a short time later was used as the basis for a painting on board by an unknown artist that hangs today in the lobby to the Parlour, in which the horizon amusingly appears to vanish at the boundaries of the College.

Loggan shows vividly the transformative impact of the Chapel and arcaded Cloister on the character and the orientation of Emmanuel. This would lead to the redevelopment of the rest of the court in the eighteenth century, but whether or not this was the original intent of Wren and Sancroft's plan we cannot know. The core of the College and general feel of the ensemble is still broadly recognisable from Loggan, despite later alterations. In the engraving, the older parts reveal their monastic origins in their uneven architectural arrangement, visible buttresses and a filled-in gothic window. Loggan's view exhibits little other evidence of work in the 1680s or 1690s, although internally the Hall's new wainscot was financed by Sir William Temple. The panelling at the dais end and screen panelling all date from the same time, being 'wainscotted, painted and new glazed' between April and October 1694.[53]

Loggan's view also clearly shows the Master's Garden east of the old Chapel (by then the Library), with the Fellows' Garden – *Hortus Sociorum* – densely planted and including a tunnel arbour, no doubt supporting scented climbers. Rows of tall trees framed the enclosed field (the Paddock) on the south and west sides. The sets of rooms in the Founder's Range and Old Court looked out onto another garden dense with trees (now Chapman's Garden), apparently on a diagonal or chequer pattern. These gardens must have been agreeable places of retreat, the trees providing visual variety and shade in the summer. The inner court (now Front Court) appears to have been handsomely railed, as does the then entrance court (now New Court) with the road-front wall to the north protected by turned posts and rails painted white.

The axis created by the rectangular Chapel running east from the inner court must have impressed itself on minds well schooled in the classical tradition as a wasted opportunity. A new entry, aligned to the Chapel door, was possibly considered by the 1740s and probably earlier, and was finally executed in the early 1770s. It was an entrance to a world that had changed both culturally and philosophically from the period in which the Chapel designed by Wren was built.

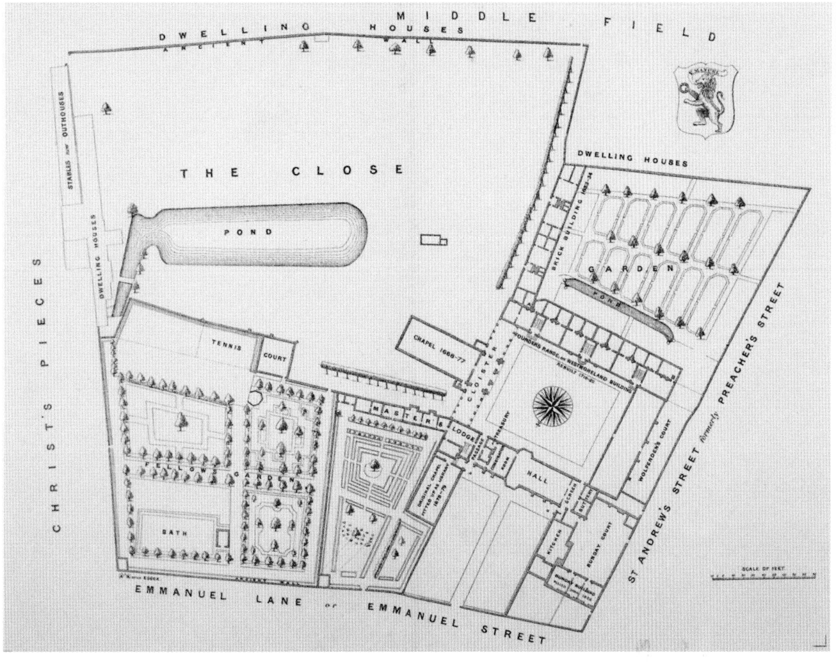

The James Essex 1746 survey of Emmanuel College (as later published by Willis and Clark 1887).

Loggan's 1688 map of Cambridge shows Emmanuel still on the edge of the town, and thus rather different in character from the medieval and Tudor colleges in the centre of the town, shown along the top of these pages. The map was published in Cantabrigia Illustrata *in 1690.*

Bridge Street
The Master of St Iohns Coll: Dove hous and fish ponds
Bowling Green
Walls Lane
Sidney Coll: Close
Iesus Close
Iesus Lane
Bow. Green
Bowling Green
Christ Coll Pe ce
Walls Lane
a pound
Iesus Close
Close
Iesus
St Peters Coll: or Peter-house
Pembroke Hall
Queens Colledge
Catharine Hall
St Bennetts or Corpus Christi Coll
Kings Colledge
Clare Hall
Trinity Hall
Gonevill & Cajus College
Trinity Colledge
St Johns Colledge
St Magdalen Colledge
Iesus Colledge
Sidney Sussex Colledge
P . Christ College
Q . Emanuel College
R . Publick Schooles & Library
1 . Kings Coll: Chappel
2 . Great St Marys Church
3 . St Michaels Church
4 . All Sts Church
5 . St Sepulchers Church
6 . St Clements Church
7 . St Gyless Church
8 . St Peters Church
9 . Trinity Church
10 . St Andrews Church
11 . St Edwards Church
12 . St Benetts Church
13 . St Butolph's Church
14 . Little St Marys Church
15 . The chief Market
16 . The pease market
17 . The hogg Market
18 . The Town Hall
19 . The Town Prison
20 . The Post house
21 . The Free Schoole
22 . The Spinn house
23 . The Almes houses
24 . Small Bridges
25 . Garret Ostle Bridge
26 . The Regent Walk
27 . St Bennets street
28 . Kings Coll: Lane
29 . Queens Coll: Lane
30 . mill Lane
31 . Little St marrys Lane
32 . Emanuel Lane
33 . Christs Coll: Lane
34 . Petty Cury
35 . Free School Lane
36 . Shoemaker Row
37 . Green street
38 . Peter-hous Garden
39 . The Tennis Courts

WILLIAM SANCROFT 1617–1693

No other figure had as significant an effect on the later seventeenth-century College as William Sancroft.[54] A nephew of a previous Master, he was born at Fressingfield in Suffolk, enrolled at Emmanuel in 1633 and became a Fellow in 1642. In 1643, 65 Cambridge Royalists, including Richard Holdsworth, Master of Emmanuel, were ejected. Sancroft was Royalist in sympathy but retained his Fellowship until he resigned in 1651, going into voluntary exile on the Continent. He was in Italy when recalled at the Restoration.

After the Bishop of Durham – John Cosin, a previous Master of Peterhouse – made him one of his chaplains (and subsequently rector of Houghton-le-Spring and a prebend of Durham Cathedral), Sancroft helped prepare the 1662 *Book of Common Prayer*. He was appointed Master of Emmanuel in 1662, and in January 1664 became Dean of York. In 1665, he resigned his Mastership following his appointment as Dean of St Paul's in November 1664, but continued to see through plans to build a new Chapel at Emmanuel orientated to the east, designed by Christopher Wren.

In 1677 he was appointed Archbishop of Canterbury, at the express wish of Charles II. Sancroft became an unlikely national hero when, in 1687, James II issued, without the authority of Parliament, his Declaration of Indulgence, offering religious and civic equality to Roman Catholics and Dissenters.[55] Sancroft with six of his bishops protested against this unconstitutional act; they were put on trial for sedition, but acquitted amid public acclamation.

Nevertheless, Sancroft felt unable to swear allegiance to William and Mary during the lifetime of the former king, James II, and in 1690 he was deprived of his archbishopric. He was ejected from Lambeth Palace and retired to his family's estate at Fressingfield where he died in 1693, not before he had doubled the Emmanuel book collection with a gift of almost his entire library of over 5,000 books.

JOHN WALLIS 1616–1703

John Wallis has been described as 'the greatest of Newton's precursors in mathematics'.[56] At an early age, he discovered that mathematics 'suited my humour so well that I did thenceforth prosecute it, not as a formal study, but as a pleasing diversion at spare hours'.

His studies were not easy, 'For I had none to direct me what books to read, or what to seek, or in what method to proceed'. At that time mathematics was viewed 'as the business of traders, merchants, seamen, carpenters, surveyors of lands and the like'.[57]

Wallis studied at Emmanuel from 1632 to 1640 and was ordained in 1640. As a private chaplain, he walked the tightrope of mid-seventeenth-century politics. While attached to the household of Lord Vere in 1642, he deciphered a secret letter, after which his codebreaking skills were much used by the Parliamentarians. He gave evidence against Archbishop Laud in 1644, but in 1649 he also signed the remonstrance against the execution of Charles I.

In 1649, Cromwell appointed him to the Savilian Professorship of Geometry at Oxford, a position he retained at the Restoration. From 1644 he was also secretary to the Westminster Assembly of Divines. He began to meet with Robert Boyle and others to discuss science, which led to the foundation of the Royal Society, an 'invisible college' of natural philosophers and physicians.[58]

The Society 'barred all discussion of Divinity, of State Affairs, and of news' so it would not be diverted from its work on 'philosophical inquiries, and related topics; as medicine, anatomy, geometry, astronomy, navigation, statics, mechanics, and natural experiments'.[59] His *Arithmetica Infinitorum* (1655) contains an exploration of what is now known as integral and differential calculus. He also wrote a book on English grammar with an appendix on the production of speech-sounds that he later developed as a method of teaching the deaf-and-dumb (as he described them in his letter to Boyle) to talk.

RACHEL, COUNTESS OF BATH 1613–1680

Rachel Fane, Countess of Bath, was a benefactor of the College and great-granddaughter of the founder, Sir Walter Mildmay.[60] She was one of the 14 children of Sir Francis Fane, later 1st Earl of Westmorland, and his wife, Mary Mildmay. In 1617, her family moved to Apethorpe in Northamptonshire along with her widowed grandmother, Mildmay's daughter-in-law, Grace.

Rachel Fane's notebooks show that she was highly educated, being well read in French, poetry and classical literature. She wrote an original but unfinished masque, performed in 1625 at Christmas. In 1638 she married Henry Bourchier, 5th Earl of Bath; they did not have any children. Lady Bath was a careful housekeeper and administrator, especially during her husband's incarceration in the Tower of London during the Civil War. In 1655, months after Lord Bath's death, Rachel married Lionel Cranfield, 3rd Earl of Middlesex. In June 1661 she obtained a separation on the grounds of cruelty and desertion, and reverted to her earlier title. In 1676–77 she gave £200 to Emmanuel College to buy books, which had commemorative plates inserted.

She died in 1680. Her memorial at St Peter's Church, Tawstock, Devon, says:

> *she had a genius exceeding that of a man, and such a motherly disposition that scarce a greater existed in the world although she was childless yet she was parent to more than a thousand children, whom in a very genteel manner she brought up, gave them portions, consecrated and even ennobled.*[61]

[opposite above] *William Sancroft, 1650, by Bernard Lens.*

[opposite below] *John Wallis, c.1640–50, by an unknown artist.*

[above] *Rachel, Countess of Bath, c.1630, by an unknown artist.*

[above right] *Sir William Temple, c.1660, after Sir Peter Lely.*

SIR WILLIAM TEMPLE 1628–1699

Sir William Temple was the son of Sir John Temple, Master of the Rolls in Ireland, and he entered Emmanuel in 1644 as a Fellow-Commoner. He clearly maintained considerable affection for the College, and in 1694 presented the dining hall with a new set of tables, which are still used today (and possibly the 'forms', or benches, too).[62]

Between 1655 and 1660 he lived in Ireland, and after the Restoration he became a diplomat, being well travelled and fluent in French and Spanish. His writing was much admired and a contemporary wrote that: 'The Style of Sir William Temple is very harmonious and sweet, full of Spirit, and Raciness of Wit, to use a Word of his own'.[63]

He played an important role in negotiating the Triple Alliance of England, Sweden and Holland to create a balance of power against France, and was instrumental in arranging the peace that ended the Second Dutch War. In 1674, Temple helped to arrange the marriage of Charles II's niece to William of Orange (later William III and Mary II). He was an influential privy councillor under Charles II until 1681, when he retired to his country estate, Moor Park, in Surrey, where he redesigned the garden, which included many new varieties of exotic fruit from abroad.

Temple famously employed Jonathan Swift as a secretary and in return, in *Gulliver's Travels*, Swift made the hero a former Emmanuel man.[64] Temple also left this advice for young men: to 'talk little, to hear much, to reflect alone upon what has passed in company, to distrust one's own opinions, and value others that deserve it'.[65]

4

On Classic Ground

The eighteenth century was an era of stability and political and social consistency, and one during which important features of the University's reputation were founded: for instance, the Mathematical Tripos.[1] But it was also a time of reducing College numbers, and average annual admissions were down to as few as nine in 1719. Between 1743 and 1766, the average number of residents, other than Fellows, including a few graduates, was 43, in sharp contrast to the total who had flocked to Emmanuel in the 1620s (when there had been over 250 undergraduates).[2]

At Emmanuel, the slightly haphazard building improvements and additions made in the classical style in the mid- to late eighteenth century became nonetheless one of the enduring, admired and defining characteristics of the College. What is now Front Court was changed in three phases during the eighteenth century, the updates probably partly aimed at attracting Fellow-Commoners, wealthier undergraduates who paid for extra privileges including dining at High Table and wearing grander gowns.

The sum of these architectural improvements was noted by one Emmanuel man, George Dyer, in 1819:

> *This* [College] *is neither so ancient, nor so large, nor so magnificent; nor is it so ample in its endowment, nor so memorable for its number, – being a younger foundation – of distinguished personages. Yet, as a building, it is elegant, without being frivolous, and various, without being crowded; and as a neat whole its elevation is, perhaps, one of the most agreeable in the University.*[3]

Over a century earlier a German bibliophile, Zacharias Conrad von Uffenbach, had visited Emmanuel in the summer of 1710 and observed with similar warmth:

> *This collegium is tolerably large, and even the back court well built [referring to the building by Wren]. In the first [court] is a library on the ground floor in a tolerably large room. The books are respectable in number ... when we had done with the library, we*

[previous pages] *A classical transformation: the Founder's Range was remodelled and refronted in the 1720s with this formal elevation, probably designed by John Lumley, a surveyor who worked for the 6th Earl of Westmorland. The inspiration for this grand reordering seems to have been to make the College more attractive to the Fellow-Commoners, wealthier undergraduates who provided the College with an essential income.*

> *went into the second court of this college, to view the chapel, which is indeed small, but neat. Before the church is a cloister, and above it a fine saloon, called the gallery, in which many portraits hang.*[4]

Further works were being planned in the early 1700s. The Founder's Building (the 1580s' southern range of the inner court, now Front Court) was considered both old-fashioned and in poor repair. A College Order of 1714–15 agreed to the suppression of two Fellowships because the income was needed for building works as 'the Walls, Roofs, and Tilings ... are much decay'd and out of Repair'.[5] In 1718, a letter of appeal for help from the Master put it a little more dramatically:

> *materials of his building proving very defective, the ruinous condition to which, notwithstanding the expense and care which have from time to time been bestow'd upon it, a great part of it is at last reduc't, obliges us to look abroad for contributions to enable us to rebuild it in a better manner...*[6]

[right] The Return of the Prodigal Son, *painted in London by the Venetian artist and scene-painter, Giacomo Amigoni (1682–1752), in 1734 and presented in the same year as an altar painting by a Fellow-Commoner, Christopher Nevile.*

Institutional reviews of this period have always tended to exaggerate conditions, scaling up from 'out of repair' to 'ruinous'. Modern analysis of the building plan and structure suggests that some of the original outside walls survive from the late sixteenth-century building. But new building ranges were important for the attraction of Fellow-Commoners who required a spacious sitting room/study and bedroom adjoining, a model made fashionable by works at New College Oxford in the 1680s and early 1700s to create the Garden Quad there, as accommodation for 'Gentleman Commoners'.[7]

In August 1719, Emmanuel resolved to pull down and rebuild, and £2,400 was raised towards the costs: Thomas Fane, 6th Earl of Westmorland, gave £500; his brother Colonel John Fane, £100.[8] The Earl appears to have offered the services of his surveyor, John Lumley, who worked at Apethorpe, Northamptonshire, designing the great orangery there.[9] The Westmorland Building, as designed by Lumley (his bill for 1719–20 noted that he 'drew the plan &c.' and he supplied a complex specification for the sash windows), was a dignified classical addition of three storeys. The masonry work was entrusted to the leading Cambridge mason Robert Grumbold, who was infirm (he died in 1720) and passed the work to his 'son', William Pitches.[10] Panelling was being installed by carpenters in 1722 including James Essex Sr, whose son we shall hear of later.

There are three doors and three staircases, and the centrepiece of the elevation is a pair of giant order Ionic pilasters, with rather refined carved capitals. This stately new building was largely completed in 1724, and the Earl and Countess of Westmorland were entertained at the College to celebrate its completion.[11] The 'Founder's Coate of Armes with inrichment Round it' was added in 1724, carved by John Woodward.[12]

During this period, the Admonition Book had its regular entries on undergraduate drunkenness, foul language and other disturbances, but it is a surprise to read on 24 August 1725 of a rather difficult Fellow: 'Memorandum that Mr Fuller Sen Fellow, & Dean of the College was Admonish'd by the Master in the presence of all the Fellows then in College for great offences that he was guilty of'.[13] Fuller's long service meant he was not dislodged, but his name appears again in November 1726:

> *Mr Fuller being summon'd, did appear before the Master & Senior Fellows & Dean, and the Master proceeded to Admonish him for his irregular behaviour & notorious neglect of duty. Upon this Admonition, he behav'd himself in a very insolent outrageous manner: & upon the Master's testimony that he admonished him according to the direction of the statutes; he reply'd A fart for your Admonition & used other contemptuous language.*[14]

Troublesome Fellows did not, however, unduly obstruct the building plans of the College. Once a college has modernised and radically improved one wing of a court, the older parts often come under greater scrutiny. By the 1740s, it was beginning to be felt that the kitchen, butteries and associated buildings on the western side of the College, adapted in the 1580s from the former Dominican priory buildings, were in need of modernisation. This need came to the attention of the amateur architect, James Burrough, of Caius College.

Burrough was the leading light of architectural improvement in mid-eighteenth-century Cambridge, working in several colleges and apparently providing the early designs for the Senate House, which was finally to pass to James Gibbs to design. A Fellow of Caius, and later Master of that college, Burrough was knighted in 1759.[15] He also assiduously brought on as his Cambridge-bred protégé the talented James Essex, who becomes significant in the story of Emmanuel – the son of James Essex Sr mentioned above. Burrough was responsible for the classicising of the Hall at Queens' and the Chapel at Corpus Christi, as well as the classical stone elevations introduced to the principal courts of Trinity Hall in the 1740s, and at Peterhouse in the 1750s, while Essex continued the process at Christ's and St John's.

In 1735, Burrough was paid by Emmanuel for 'his assistance in beautifying the chappell'.[16] The chandelier had been presented in 1732, later described as 'a curious glass chandelier, which has a very beautiful appearance when lighted'.[17] It is possible that Burrough designed the plasterwork at the centre of the ceiling.[18] Although the detail of his 1735 work is not recorded it may also have included the installation of the altar painting by Venetian artist Jacopo Amigoni, who worked in London from 1729 to 1739. It is a depiction of *The Return of the Prodigal Son*, the gift of a Fellow-Commoner, Christopher Nevile. The subject is unusual and there has been much debate about whether it symbolises penitence, or the importance of the Eucharist (by virtue of the killing of the fatted calf to celebrate the son's return), or even, perhaps, the end of the Puritan experiment.[19] It could also have been an acknowledgement of fashionable Grand Tour taste, the tour being a period of Continental travel that gave wealthy Englishmen greater knowledge of the arts and appreciation of the classical.

Another reflection of this tradition of travel might be the scented planting installed around the cold bath and pool that were added to the Fellows' Garden in 1745, bringing with them a whiff of Continental tastes.[20] Adjacent to the bathing pool, a small classical summerhouse (for changing in) was added, apparently with a plunge bath below.[21] Although some aspects

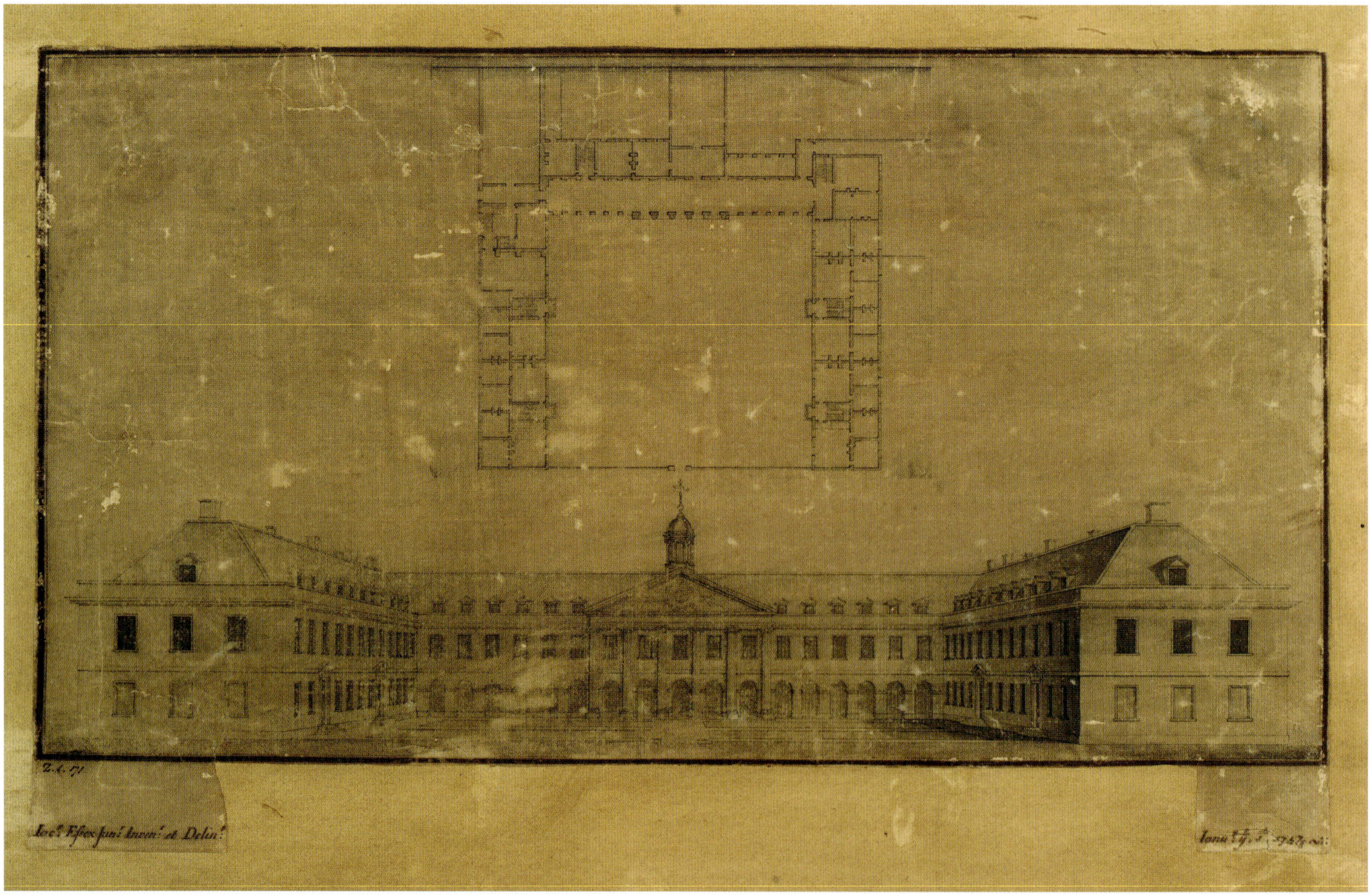

[above] *A 1748 proposal for the remodelling of the College, which envisaged the demolition of the Elizabethan western range, the rebuilding of the northern and southern ranges, and the extension and addition of another storey on the Chapel and Gallery range. Although signed by James Essex, the character is very close in spirit to the work of Sir James Burrough. The Cloister, anti-Chapel and Chapel are all still clearly visible at the top of the plan.*

[previous pages] *The Founder's Building was mostly rebuilt in the 1720s (and rechristened the Westmorland Building after the descendant of the Founder who contributed generously to the building fund), and extended the classical grandeur of the court, still then approached from the north, via the Hall. The proportions of the new range did not follow those of Wren's building.*

have changed, the present stone coping around the pool seems to be that supplied in 1745.[22]

The desire to update and remodel Emmanuel in classical spirit proved almost irresistible. In the British Library is a design dated 1748, which is drawn up and signed, 'Inv[eni]t et Delin[eavi]t' [designed and drawn] James Essex, but it bears the hallmarks of an idea by Burrough. This design proposed a radical reformation of Emmanuel's inner court, now Front Court.[23] This extraordinary (but happily never pursued) proposal would have entirely removed the western range, where the main entrance is now, to create a three-sided court facing west. The Chapel was to be retained after a fashion but an extra attic floor added to the Gallery, and the frontispiece enlarged to five rather than three bays and the pediment widened accordingly.

Bizarrely, the relatively recently completed Westmorland Building would have had to have been peeled down a floor, or rather the third storey converted into an attic storey, and the facing range, the Hall (medieval in origin and repurposed in the 1580s), entirely replaced with accommodation in a matching design. It was a very ambitious but not wholly comfortable compromise. There seems to have been no formal request for these designs in the College Order Book, but Burrough may have been in private dialogue with the Master, William Richardson, an energetic, strong-willed figure. The vision expressed in this design was certainly for a grander, more publicly visible, set of buildings, reflecting the thinking of a leading Cambridge figure about how a college should be modernised: moving away from enclosed, secretive medieval compounds to something more permeable, open and grand.

This set of drawings in the British Library records both projects for which James Essex served Burrough and some other, later, projects, which he did in his own right. While Essex boldly asserts authorship in the signature, and, as we will see, in the 1770s came to build a new western range, it must be said that the character of this British Library proposal is very close in spirit to Burrough's 1740s' proposals for Trinity Hall in Cambridge, which were equally radical and only partly realised.[24] But then the two were certainly 'not only like-minded but in such close contact that even on the day Burrough died Essex had been with him discussing business'.[25]

Sir James Burrough's 1743 radical proposal for the remodelling of Trinity Hall Cambridge, with an open classical court facing the River Cam. The plan was not executed and would have required the demolition of the late sixteenth-century Library and Master's Lodge.

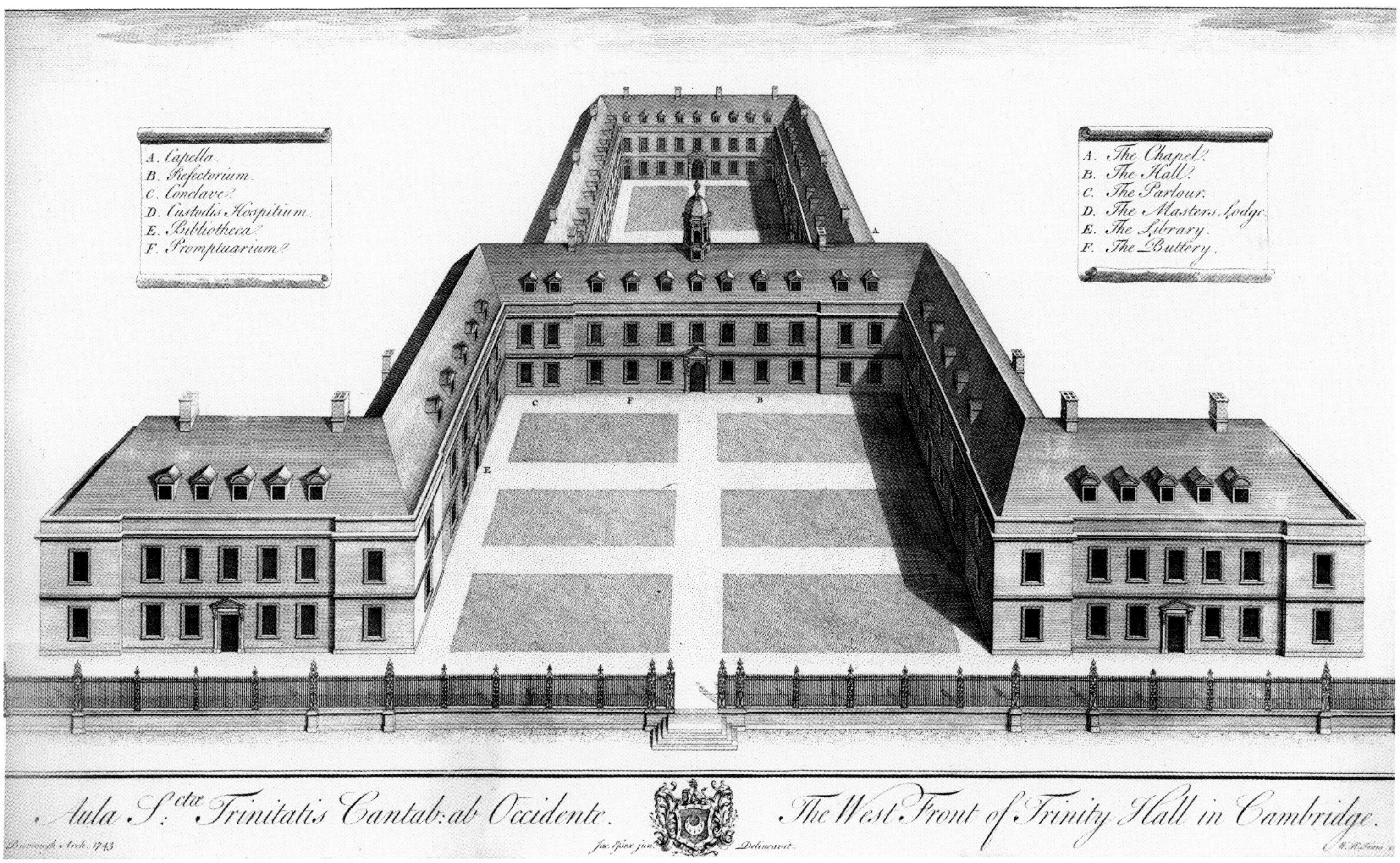

The Hall looking eastwards. James Essex inserted a flat ceiling to conceal the open Elizabethan roof structure and to carry a compartmented ceiling with rococo plasterwork decoration.

Curiously, the College Order Book does not mention any discussions about works to the College in 1748, but in 1752 it was Burrough who was named as the architect involved in developing ideas for the College. He was directly mentioned when it was recorded:

> *the Butteries and contiguous Buildings are become very ruinous, and it is hop'd that Benefactions may be procur'd to defray the expence ... Agreed that they be pull'd down and rebuilt so soon as money sufficient be rais'd for that purpose; & that the Butteries and the end rooms in Bungay court be the first that be gone upon.*[26] [Bungay court was a small extension between the kitchen range and the street.]

It was agreed that 'Mr Burrough to be desir'd to prepare a plan for the whole of the said intended new Building in conformity to that call'd the Founder's Range.' This must have been for a new building facing the Chapel on the west side of the Court, but this design does not survive, nor was it carried out, although it may have helped establish the principles of the rebuilding that followed in the 1760s and 1770s.

There were other plans for College improvements too. The highly active – and married – Master, Richardson, distinguished antiquary and chaplain to the king, found his Lodge far too small and sought to incorporate the Parlour into it. This clearly put him at odds with the Fellowship and, although he was a man of vigour and enterprise, it was a battle he lost. Fellow William Bennet recorded that Richardson proposed to have the 'present Combination Room added to his Lodge, and the passage between them stop'd up. The fellows on the other hand were unwilling to go to the bottom of the hall to a more distant and noisy room.'[27]

It was all a bit embarrassing and money raised for the project had to be returned but the issue of the Lodge was a recurring problem, partly because of the modesty of the original provision, even with the addition of the Gallery. A series of Masters had made small improvements, including a suite of rooms extending east from the main building that appears in the 1746 survey (see p. 77), but not in Loggan's view from the late 1680s, which were probably kitchens and pantries with bedrooms above.[28]

The Hall looking westwards, from Rudolf Ackerman's, History of the University of Cambridge *(1815), showing the 1690s' screen with the ceiling introduced by James Essex in 1760–64.*

Whether or not Burrough advised on this we do not know (he died in 1764), but Essex had certainly been called in to update the Hall and improve its presence in the Court. From 1760 to 1764 this was refaced with ashlar and given a new parapet to mirror that of the Westmorland Building (the parapet also changed the visual relationship of the Hall range and the Gallery). Inside Essex fitted a flat ceiling decorated with fashionable rococo plasterwork, and elegant wrought-iron gates to his design were also inserted into the screen at the west end. He laid a Ketton stone floor (removed in the 1860s) and updated the interior of the Parlour.

Essex did his best for the College, especially in the western range, which in the end was left to him to rebuild. One late eighteenth-century guidebook to Cambridge recognised his achievement:

> *On the west, next the street, is erected a very handsome building … which make[s] the principal court a very beautiful one, having on the south an elegant uniform stone building, adorned with a balustrade and parapet; and opposite to it, on the north, the hall, combination-room, and Master's Lodge; on the east is a fine cloister with 13 arches, and an handsome gallery over it, well-furnished and adorned with portraits.*[29]

Portrait of the Georgian joiner and architect James Essex who worked on the Hall, Front Court and new west range at Emmanuel College, and on St John's, Trinity and Queens'.

The 1670s' Chapel was still a star attraction:

> *In the middle of the cloister is the entrance into the chapel … extremely well adorned and furnished … The hall is one of the most elegant in the university, having been fitted up in a grand taste; the carved work, wainscoting, and fret-work of the ceiling being highly finished … The gardens are extensive and pleasant, with a bowling green.*[30]

This reaction reflects the charming setting and the admired up-to-dateness of Essex's contributions. By the mid-1760s, three sides of the main court had been updated and become classical, albeit to different degrees. After this, it was hardly surprising that the final unmodernised range, which formed the western part, was considered in need of rebuilding. In March 1769, the Order Book notes:

> *the building opposite the chapel is in so ruinous a condition that the Surveyor says that it can stand but very few years, agreed that the butteries and the building running from thence to the street, be immediately pulled down and rebuilt according to the plan drawn by Sir James Burrough some years hence.*[31]

This might possibly refer to the design (signed by Essex) that survives from 1748, but it should be noted that this proposal,

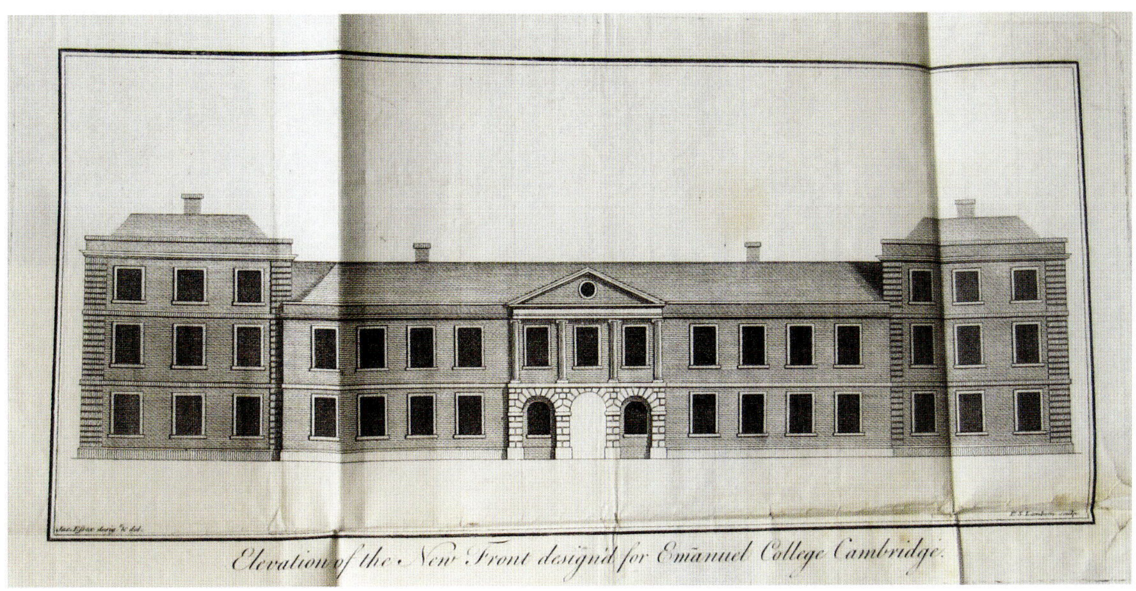

James Essex's first design for the rebuilding of the western range of Emmanuel College, which was engraved in February 1771 and sent out with a letter seeking funds for the project, with a different version of the centrepiece then built. The design included a new principal entrance.

The College seen from the south-west in the 1830s, along St Andrew's Street, with the giant Ionic engaged columns of the centrepiece, which help to balance the awkward proportions of the elevation and the different heights of the buildings in the court behind. Drawn by R.B. Harraden and etched by Elizabeth Byrne.

in effect, had no west range at all, or it could refer to another related to the recorded 1752 request, which Essex had drawn up on Burrough's behalf.[32]

The work of the new west range was certainly put in the hands of Essex, who had gradually been 'promoted' by Burrough while running his own family joinery business and building a reputation as an antiquary. Essex became especially well known for his knowledge of gothic architecture, and in the 1760s was active in works to both Ely and Lincoln Cathedrals, and in the 1770s provided the ambitious plan for a new reredos treatment for the east end of King's College Chapel, which survived *in situ* until the early twentieth century.[33]

Essex became a friend of Horace Walpole, introduced by the Cambridge antiquary, William Cole, and in the 1770s he designed a significant addition to Walpole's gothic revival house, Strawberry Hill: the Beauclerk Tower, as well as the office range. In the same decade, he also designed the handsome neoclassical Combination Room for Trinity College.[34] Of Essex's work at Emmanuel, the usually perceptive and accurate Bennet (himself an eminent antiquary) noted 'the plan of Sir James Burrough [was] departed from in almost every instance, and in some [instances] considerably improved', but again we cannot be sure to which design Bennet referred.[35]

Essex's new plan was approved by the College Order of 5 July 1769, which stated: 'agreed that the Plan drawn by Mr Essex for rebuilding the West side of the Court be carried into Execution, when the College shall be enabled to do it'.[36] When funds were secured, the medieval and Elizabethan building facing the Chapel was demolished and replaced by the two-storey range that we see today. One of Essex's later designs survives: an engraved version (see p. 93) that appeared in February 1771 printed on a letter sent out seeking funds.[37] It has the same general outline but a different pedimented centrepiece framing the new entrance, with a rather compressed two-storey neo-Palladian arrangement with engaged columns applied to the first floor only, different from the giant order Ionic engaged columns as executed.

What is so striking about Essex's work is the deliberate lowness of the centre of the west range, which might seem surprising given the opportunity to create a three-storey range with additional accommodation. This reticence may have been informed by economy, but there might also have been more aesthetic issues at play if Essex was seeking, either with advice or on his own initiative, to complete a courtyard range that did proper homage to the Chapel and Gallery range designed by Wren. Essex, in completing Burrough's Chapel for Clare College to his own revised designs, also seems there to have made a subtle homage to Wren's west face of Pembroke College in the east elevation of Clare's Chapel.[38]

This choice of scale in turn had obvious challenges for Essex, as Emmanuel's new entrance range's two-storey height made it hard to design a centrepiece of sufficient size, but the 'giant order' Ionic engaged columns (running the height of two storeys) improved the feel. The central arch naturally creates a visual focus on the Chapel door, and the covered walkway and colonnade of the western range add to the character of the court. In the 1780s, Bennet even called the entrance range 'the Cloyster building', which again suggests an imaginative link between the west range and the east range designed by Wren, with its spacious covered way under the Gallery, known as the Cloister.[39]

Although there is no direct documentary evidence, it seems not unreasonable to suggest that Essex, a well-informed antiquary, relished the significance of Wren in the story of English architecture and wished to protect the court's character. Wren's inclusion in Colen Campbell's *Vitruvius Britannicus* (1716) illustrates that he was rated as of national significance by the early eighteenth-century neo-Palladians.[40]

The tower-ended outline of the Emmanuel entrance range might also be compared with the design for the King's Building

[following pages] *Looking westwards towards the entrance range, showing the building as designed by James Essex, to reflect and honour the Cloister and Chapel range designed by Wren in 1769–70. The commitment to a two-storey building may have been intentional, preserving the proportion of the court appropriate to Wren's building.*

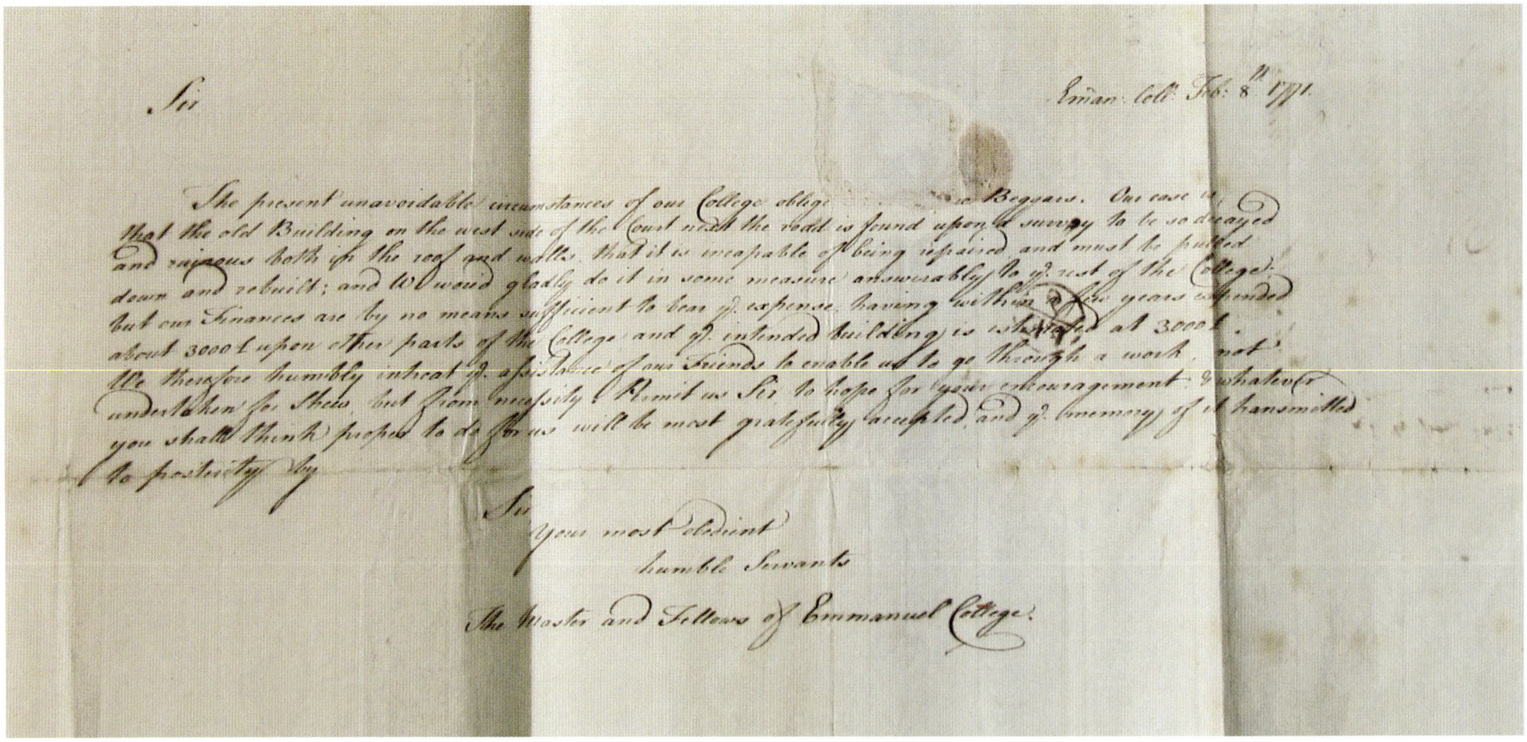

Sir

Eman: Coll: Feb: 8th 1771.

The present unavoidable circumstances of our College oblige [illegible] Beggars. Our case is that the old Building on the west side of the Court next the road is found upon a survey to be so decayed and ruinous both in the roof and walls, that it is incapable of being repaired and must be pulled down and rebuilt; and We would gladly do it in some measure answerably to ye rest of the College: but our Finances are by no means sufficient to bear ye expense, having within [illegible] years expended about 3000l upon other parts of the College and ye intended building is estimated at 3000l. We therefore humbly intreat ye assistance of our Friends to enable us to go through a work, not undertaken for Shew, but from necessity. Permit us Sir to hope for your encouragement; & whatever you shall think proper to do for us will be most gratefully accepted, and ye memory of it transmitted to posterity by

Sir
Your most obedient
humble Servants
The Master and Fellows of Emmanuel College.

The text of the February 1771 letter sent out by the College to raise funds for the new west range.

at Greenwich, also published in *Vitruvius Britannicus*, created by John Webb in the 1630s but absorbed into Wren's master plan and matched with a new building to form the open-sided riverside court of the Greenwich Hospital.[41] This was the kind of reference work that Essex would have owned. This is not to suggest that Emmanuel's building was a replica, as the scales are entirely different, only that it may have given Essex the idea for his unusual composition.

Essex's design was, in effect, a bold attempt to resolve a difficult issue as carefully as he could. For had Essex designed (or been asked to design) a three-storey range on this side, or even a two-storey one with habitable attic, the Chapel and Gallery group would have been effectively dwarfed, and entirely lost its visual status. The plain, east-facing arcade of the new entrance range echoes the more ornate arcade of Wren's Gallery.

When the letter in search of funds was sent out, among others Richard Hurd, then Archdeacon of Gloucester (formerly a Fellow of Emmanuel), sent £50. In his reply, Hurd added: 'A less formal intimation of their pleasure, from yourself, or any of my other friends, would have been abundantly sufficient. My great obligations to your worthy Society, & the singular respect I must ever bear to it, make me a willing contributor to so good and necessary a work'.[42]

Richardson wrote to thank him on 16 February 1771, explaining the formality was because the letter was issued while he was away at Bath for his health, but the matter was pressing:

When the old Building was surveyed, the Report was that it might stand three or four years, but that he (the Surveyor) would not live in it one. We therefore began to pull down immediately; & have rebuilt the Buttery end, to answer the other, upon our own strength, at £1000 Expense. The middle must come down this Spring: But as you know that our Finances will not furnish 3000 more, we are forc'd to be troublesom[e] to our Friends ... [43]

The 'troublesomeness' paid off, and the new building was completed by May 1775.[44]

Bennet generously observed: 'when the great repairs of the hall, chapel and now of the front or cloyster building (in all which £10,000 was expended) are consider'd, it reflects the highest honour on Dr Richardson's Mastership, whose economy in college affairs provided the funds, and whose good sense directed the expenditure'. He was otherwise uncomplimentary about Richardson's officiousness as Master, 'He was a most strict and unpleasant Master to his Fellows, but had a great regard for the prosperity of the Body, with a Gentleman-like behaviour, and liberal mind.'[45] These new comfortable spaces were no doubt greatly enjoyed by the more convivial – but rather less efficient – Richard Farmer, Master from 1775 to 1797, who had come up to Emmanuel in 1753 and been elected a Fellow in 1759. He cemented his name as a scholar with the publication of *An Essay on the Learning of Shakespeare* in 1767. His learning was unusual, especially in older English literature, 'such reading as was never read' as he described it to Dr Samuel Johnson.[46]

In fact, Farmer's reputation prompted Johnson's only known visit to Cambridge in 1765.[47] James Boswell recounted their 'joyous evening' with Johnson challenging Farmer on abstruse topics and Farmer returning such quick answers that Johnson cried: 'Gi' me your hand! Gi' me your hand! ... You are a man after my own heart'.[48]

Farmer's account of the same visit to Thomas Percy had a slightly different spin,

Since I last heard from you, I have had the unexpected pleasure of Mr Johnson's Company at Cambridge – a Character the most extraordinary, that it has ever been my fortune to meet with ... his hours are not very Academic and I have been obliged to work double tides ever since.[49]

Under Farmer, Emmanuel's Parlour became the social hub of the University: 'as Sunday was the usual day for visiting the University, persons of any station or literary acquirement would have considered their visit incomplete unless they shared in the hospitalities of Emmanuel Parlour after having dined with the Vice-Chancellor'.[50]

The wager books kept in the Parlour give some flavour of its life and conversation: 1770: 'Lord North will resign before next Michaelmas'. 1779: 'No place whatever in America (except Canada) in the hands of the Loyalists, by March 17, 1780'. 1780: 'A naval engagement between Rodney and the French, in which the latter are beaten, on or before June 30, 1781'. 1792: 'November 13. The King of France will be condemned, but not executed'. And 1794: 'April 30 and May 3. The war will be over in two years.[51]

An account of a visit in 1784 from Gerhard Wenderborn, a German scholar, reveals rather more of Farmer's character as a scholar and host, and also how the gardens complemented the libraries,

He at first received me somewhat coldly, as a stranger; but when we had spoken together for ten minutes, he took me by the arm, went with me into the College garden, showed me his own library as well as that of the College, and when he found that I desired to see the University Library at once went with me to it through several streets in his slippers, gave me a general view of it, and instructed the superintendent to have books and manuscripts which I wished to see sent to the hotel where I had put up.[52]

The garden they visited was presumably the Fellows' Garden, described by Edmund Carter in 1753 as 'very agreeable, and kept in excellent order, which, together with the Bath, Bowling-Green and Summer-House make it a little paradice [*sic*]'.[53] Wenderborn's entertainment did not end in the Library:

in the afternoon I had to eat with him and the Fellows of the College in their 'Hall' or great dining room, and afterwards spent several evenings with him in the Combination-room ... They were merry evenings, and Dr Farmer, a learned and good-humoured man, made them very pleasant by his conversation, his wit, and his joviality.[54]

Farmer died in 1797, the end of his long, avuncular reign bringing the College to the brink of a new century (for which he had notably left the College accounts in chaos).

[above] *Richard Farmer, 1784, by George Romney.*

[opposite] *Thomas Young, by an unknown artist, the 1822 original by Sir Thomas Lawrence.*

RICHARD FARMER 1735–1797

One of the finest of the College's eighteenth-century portraits is George Romney's study of Richard Farmer. Dressed in doctoral robes, with a quizzical, slightly distant look, he is the epitome of a gentleman don. Born the son of a woolman and maltster, Farmer was educated at the Free Grammar School in Leicester and came to Emmanuel as a pensioner in 1753. He was elected as a Fellow of the College in 1759, became a Fellow of the Society of Antiquaries in 1761 and of the Royal Society in 1791.[55] He was a preacher at the Chapel Royal, Whitehall, and later a canon of St Paul's Cathedral. He appears to have twice turned down offers of bishoprics, as he believed he would have made only a 'very indifferent bishop'.[56]

Farmer served Emmanuel variously as tutor, lecturer, Dean and finally as Master from 1775 to his death. He was Vice-Chancellor of the University in 1775–76 and in 1787–88; he was appointed University Librarian in 1778. An admired scholar, his expertise lay in early English literature. His sole publication, *An Essay on the Learning of Shakespeare* (1767), was written in the form of a letter to a friend, opening with: 'I have not time to teach with precision: be contented therefore with a few cursory observations, as they may happen to arise from the Chaos of Papers you have so often laughed at'.[57]

Farmer championed the study of English history and is today recognised for the assistance he gave to a wide circle of scholars. The Parlour at Emmanuel was 'always open to those who loved pipes and cheerful conversation'.[58] Farmer was a member of three London clubs: the Eumelean, the Unincreasable and the Literary Club, the last founded by his friends Joshua Reynolds and Samuel Johnson. His affable reputation as a priest was affectionately mocked in this description:

> *He began the service punctually at the appointed time, and gave a plain practical sermon, strongly enforcing some moral duty ... After morning service, he repaired to the public-house, where a mutton chop and potatoes were soon set before him: these were quickly despatched.* [He would then say to his churchwarden and assembled farmers]: *'I am going to read prayers, but shall be back by the time you have made the punch'.*[59]

THOMAS YOUNG 1773–1829

Thomas Young was an undoubted polymath and one of the most remarkable scholars to attend Emmanuel College.[60] He enrolled as a Fellow-Commoner in 1797, because Richard Farmer was a friend of his uncle, Richard Brocklesby. At that time Busick Harwood, Cambridge's most distinguished medical scholar and a renowned lecturer on anatomy, was also a Fellow.

Young is best known today as the father of the wave theory to explain how light travels – in waves and not particles – making an analogy between the transmission of sound and of light. As Frank Stubbings wrote: 'an attractive tradition has it that he first observed the phenomenon of "interference" in the ripples set up by two swans on the Emmanuel pond', which is a pleasing link between the Paddock's fish pond (a relic of the pre-foundation monastic era) and one of the most important scientific breakthroughs of the late Georgian era.[61]

Young also produced the first convincing account of colour vision, recognising that the three primary colours correspond to the retina's three receptors for different frequencies of light. Young was elected to a Fellowship of the Royal Society at the age of 21. He studied medicine in London, Edinburgh and Göttingen, before enrolling at Emmanuel in 1797 as a necessary step to getting into the Royal College of Physicians. He stayed for three years, although it seems he pursued a course of study of his own devising. In 1800, after inheriting a property in Park Lane, London, he set himself up as a physician but continued to study and publish (mostly anonymously) on scientific subjects. He was appointed Professor of Natural Philosophy at the Royal Institution and in 1814 began work on decoding the hieroglyphs of the Rosetta Stone, a process completed by Jean-François Champollion in 1822.[62]

Young's intellectual range was phenomenal: he worked on the measurement of the size of molecules and is thought to have been the first to define the word 'energy' as a scientific concept. A constant in the mathematical equation describing elasticity is named 'Young's modulus'. His epitaph in Westminster Abbey proclaims him a man 'alike eminent in almost every department of human learning'.[63]

5

A Changing Horizon

Cambridge changed considerably in the nineteenth century, and so did Emmanuel. After the Royal Commissions of 1850 and 1872, all colleges expanded and admissions to Emmanuel nearly tripled. There was a reassessment of what colleges were for, and what was researched and taught.[1] But, as with the nation at large, the pace of progress stimulated fresh conflicts over authority, and the relationship between inherited traditions and new ideas.

From the early nineteenth century, more buildings were needed to accommodate students and chapels were required to provide up-to-date places of worship. A growing spirit of historicism meant that gothic revival or Old English dress was often chosen for new buildings, with gothic the obvious choice for chapels. The rise of this style in the 1820s and 1830s had both intellectual and aesthetic inspirations, and an association with the renewed religious temperament of the age.

In Daniel and Samuel Lysons's *Magna Britannia: Cambridgeshire* (1808), Emmanuel was still described as consisting 'chiefly of one court'.[2] One Tudor-gothic-style range was added to Emmanuel in the 1820s, forming the northern arm of what became known as New Court.[3] The first plan had been to adjoin Old Court, but the architect, Charles Humfrey, may himself have suggested a new court closing the old entrance court, which once opened to Emmanuel Street.[4] Like James Essex, Humfrey was Cambridge born and bred. He is also remembered today as the architect of the finest neo-classical terraces in the city, including the grey-brick Park Terrace that overlooks Parker's Piece: two terraces, a pair of semi-detached houses and two detached villas, acquired by the College in 1983 (now in effect forming its stately southern boundary).[5]

New Court provided commodious and comfortable sets of rooms in the collegiate tradition and created a courtyard with a fashionable atmosphere of being an ancient place of learning. The new three-storey range housed 18 sets in all, approached by three staircases.[6] Each half landing has a separate staircase that

[previous pages] *View westwards from the Hostel building looking across the Paddock and pond, towards Old Court and the Chapel.*

originally served as access for gyps (college menservants, of a footman-valet type) to each room set: the arched alcoves of these second-floor gyp staircases have a distinct echo of the work of John Soane.[7] The principal room of each set faces south towards the Hall and the windows of the smaller rooms look north onto Emmanuel Street.

Charles Humfrey's gothic revival work (in the Tudor-gothic or Perpendicular style) followed the *bravura* lead of William Wilkins in the 1820s at Corpus Christi, King's and New Court at Trinity College: projects that transformed the character of Cambridge.[8] Humfrey had provided designs for Sidney Sussex, although the gothic treatment of that College was put into the hands of Jeffry Wyatville. Humfrey had already served Emmanuel College, as he had been called in to advise on the

[above] *The College from the south-west, with the 1820s' Tudor-gothic-style kitchen rebuilt to designs of a little-known architect called Arthur Brown, painted by Richard Bankes Hawarden.*

reconstruction of the Westmorland Building after a devastating fire in 1811.

A plan in the College Archives shows Humfrey offering suggestions for making the sets in the Westmorland Building more spacious in the reconstruction (see p. 106), which would have required the removal of the early eighteenth-century staircases (how much had survived the fire we cannot know).[9] These plans were rejected and the range rebuilt precisely as it had been before the fire, perhaps for reasons of cost, terms of insurance or typical Cambridge conservatism.

Humfrey's 'New Court' range also served to screen the Hall and Library from the public highway, and was followed by work on the still largely Elizabethan kitchens. These were recased in a complementary neo-Tudor style by the builder James Webster, designed by an otherwise unknown architect called Arthur Brown.[10]

This work was done under the Mastership of Robert Towerson Cory, who had succeeded Richard Farmer as Master in 1791 and held the office until his death in 1835.[11] John Barber Scott, a Fellow-Commoner in 1810, described Cory as 'timid, unused to the world, troublesomely [and] doubtfully conscientious, but very kindly disposed'.[12] He was Vice-Chancellor of the University in 1797–98 and 1813–14. There was a further degree of re-landscaping in the early and middle parts of the century and the small classical brick building near to the cold bath was replaced with a picturesque thatched changing room in a rustic spirit, probably associated with the works referenced in a College Order of 1855 (see p. 111).[13]

The next wave of building at Emmanuel belongs to rather later in the nineteenth century, by which time Tudor-gothic

Charles Humfrey's design for the north range, known as New Court, in the Tudor-gothic style, which is as executed.

The first-floor gyp staircase, which originally gave access to the gyp room, on the north side of the range. The style of the opening has echoes of the work of John Soane.

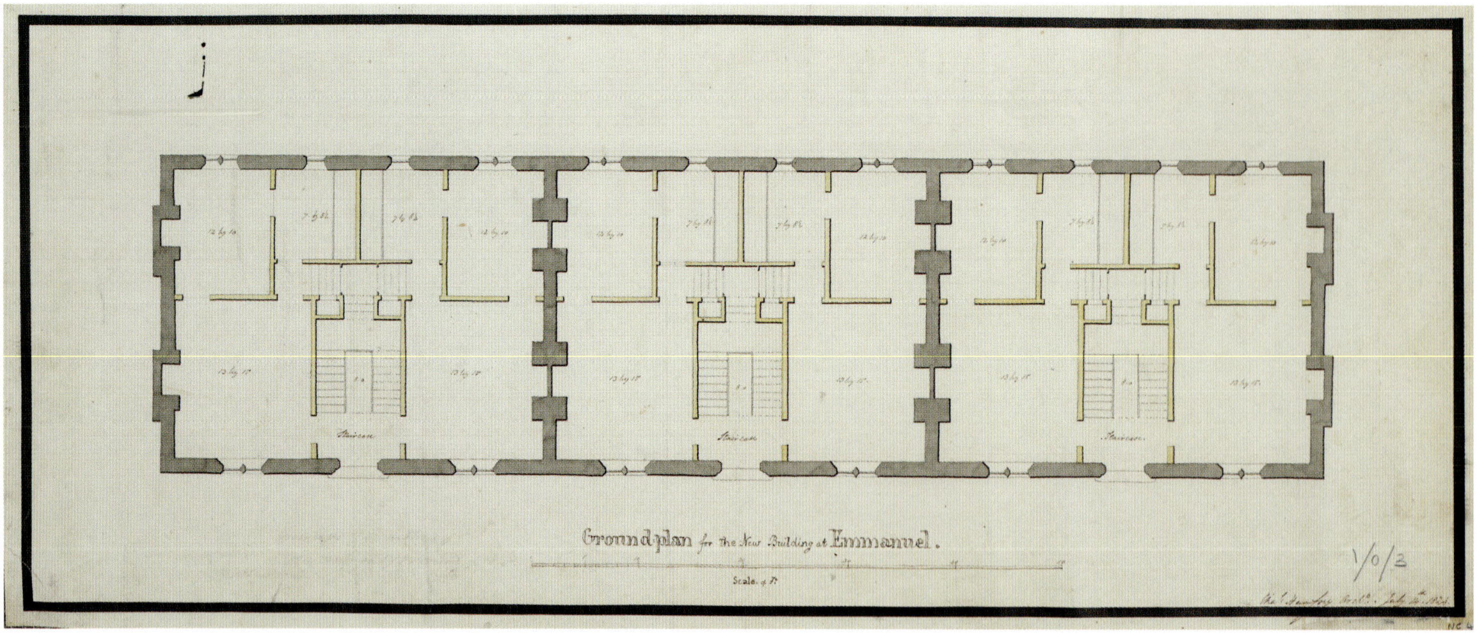

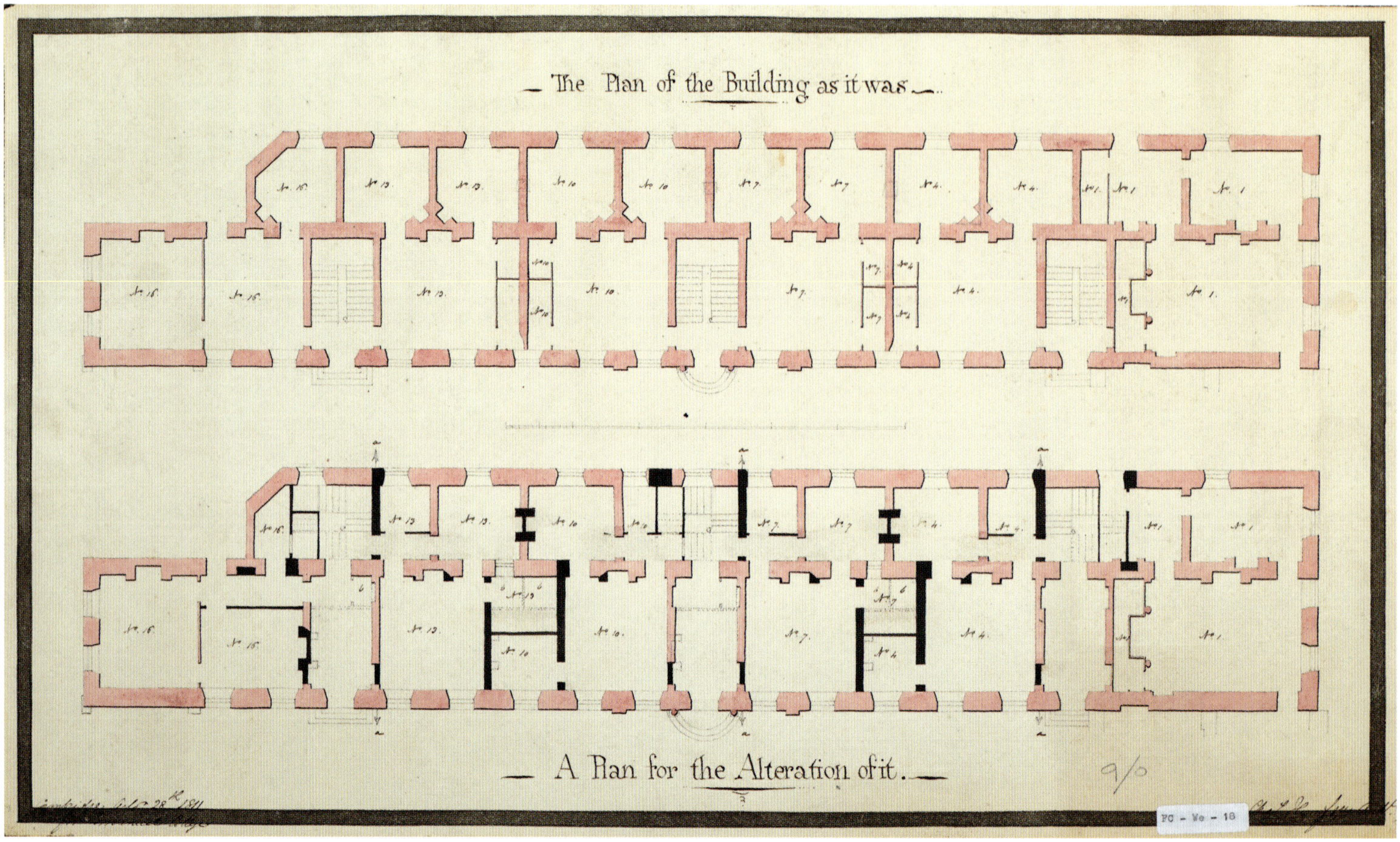

[top] *Charles Humfrey's plan of New Court, July 1824, showing the generous room sets, arranged in the traditional Cambridge manner around the staircases.*

[above] *Humfrey's rejected plan for the reordering of the Westmorland Building after the fire of 1811.*

[opposite] *The Tudor-gothic-style New Court in 2017.*

Park Terrace, designed by Charles Humfrey and built from 1831 onwards, the best early nineteenth-century set piece of Cambridge's streetscape, consisting of two terraces, with a semi-detached pair in between, and two villas (one at each end).

style had fallen out of favour. These new works were associated with the long Mastership of the Revd Samuel George Phear, best remembered as one of the founders of the Cavendish Laboratory. During his time in office College admissions rose nearly threefold.[14] Phear was a Fellow of Emmanuel from 1853, and served both as Bursar and Senior Tutor before he was elected Master in 1871 (he was Vice-Chancellor of the University in 1874 and 1875). Illness required him to stand down from the Mastership in 1895.

In the 1870s, the most significant debates about the future concerned a different kind of expansion: the relative size of a college and its buildings, the challenging economics of running a college, and how to attract good undergraduates. The Fellows hotly debated the possibility of a merger with another college and an ambitious approach to its near neighbour, Christ's, initially looked promising.[15] A College resolution of 13 June 1878 for creating 'The New College of Christ's and Emmanuel' was carried with no opposition. James Cartmell, Master of Christ's, was to be the first Master and Phear Vice-Master, with

An engraving of the Tudor-gothic-style kitchen range of Emmanuel College, facing St Andrew's Street and linking Essex's front with Humfrey's New Court range, the style of which it followed.

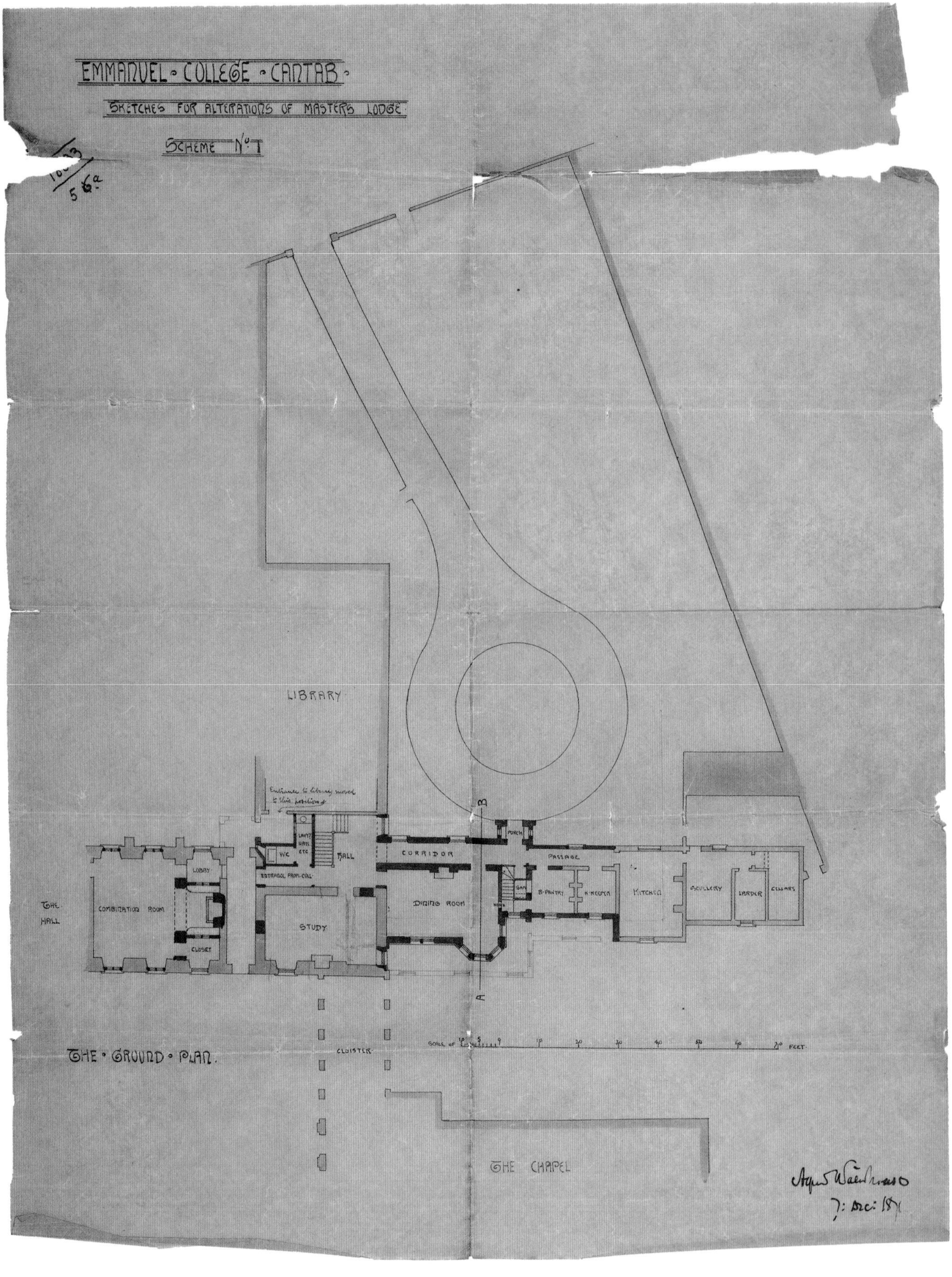
EMMANUEL · COLLEGE · CANTAB ·
SKETCHES FOR ALTERATIONS OF MASTER'S LODGE
SCHEME No. I
LIBRARY
Entrance to library moved to this position
PORCH
B
A
LAVY HAT ETC
WC
HALL
CORRIDOR
PASSAGE
ENTRANCE FROM COLL
LOBBY
THE HALL
COMBINATION ROOM
CLOSET
STUDY
DINING ROOM
B-PANTRY
H-KEEPER
KITCHEN
SCULLERY
LARDER
CELLARS
CLOISTER
THE · GROUND · PLAN
SCALE OF
FEET
THE CHAPEL

an agreement that he would succeed as the second Master of the combined college. Cartmell, however, opposed the project, and it foundered.

Alterations to buildings had carried on anyway. In early February 1872, Phear invited the architect Alfred Waterhouse into Emmanuel to advise on the restoration of the Hall and Library.[16] Waterhouse was also asked to draw up plans for remodelling the Master's Lodge.[17] One of the leading national architects at work in Cambridge, Waterhouse had already completed his partly French-Renaissance-inspired remodelling of Caius College in 1868–70, and had worked on other projects, including the design of Girton College. His landmark Manchester Town Hall was also still under construction, and in 1873 building began on London's Natural History Museum, which is probably his best-known work.[18]

Waterhouse's letter of 7 December 1871 reveals the awkwardness of Emmanuel's Master's Lodge. He had been called in,

> *in order to ascertain whether it would be practicable to carry out certain alterations which it was felt would be desirable … to improve the aspect of the Dining Room, and both aspect and arrangement of the Drawing Room, and to provide a back staircase and improve the front one.*[19]

The list seems almost tongue-in-cheek, as does his following remark that 'The House I find is contrived so curiously … considerable alterations will, I believe, be necessary'.

Waterhouse thought the main thing would be to reorder the house to allow for a dining room on the ground floor facing south over the water, and suggested creating on the first floor: 'a Drawing Room of the same size as the Dining Room, and commanding, I comprehend a beautiful south view over the water'. Nor is it surprising that, by the end of the same letter, Waterhouse adds, 'I have therefore ventured to make a sketch of an altogether New Lodge' on a slightly different site, not connecting with the older courts. He tried to make his proposal even more enticing by observing he could make space for 'four additional sets of rooms and a Lecture Room besides on the site of the present Lodge'.[20]

In the same letter, Waterhouse also gave his views on how they could improve the Combination Room: 'It doubtless would be of great advantage to throw the two stories into one and make the windows contiguous'.[21] His sketch for the new Lodge sadly does not survive in the archives, and it is not clear why the College did not pursue the plans he put forward.

Waterhouse was confident and often visionary, but he frequently preferred to build new rather than restore. In the 1870s, he rebuilt a large part of Pembroke College, but by the end of the decade he was dismissed because some Fellows there considered his work just too unsympathetic to the historic buildings. In 1879, he wrote to them: 'I gather from the [Pembroke] Treasurer's letter that it is my failure to be conservative enough which has chiefly led the College to dispense with my

[opposite] *An unexecuted proposal by Alfred Waterhouse dated 1871 for remodelling the Master's Lodge at Emmanuel. Note how he was also proposing to reorder radically the Fellows' Parlour, including moving the fireplace back and removing most of the supporting wall.*

[left] *View of the Swimming Bath, with its mid-nineteenth-century changing hut, photograph by Alfred Rose,* c.*1890.*

The staircase tower at the western end of the Hall range may have been designed by Alfred Waterhouse. Although no plans or payments survive, the treatment of the masonry can be compared with that of his work at Gonville and Caius College.

humble services for the future'.[22] George Gilbert Scott Jr, who restored (and extended by one bay) the Chapel at Pembroke in 1879–81, represented a rising younger generation who worked in much greater sympathy with the medieval and non-medieval without trying to rebuild.

But in the early 1870s Waterhouse was the architect of the moment, and one feature of Emmanuel that may possibly be credited to him is the staircase turret in the south-eastern corner of New Court, which gives access to the Gallery, as well as to the room over the Old Library and other sets of rooms that formed part of the Master's Lodge in the early 1870s. The unexpected verticality of the design and, more especially, the distinctive banding and chasing of the masonry, can be related to the stonework of the entrance of Gonville and Caius.[23]

By 18 March 1872 Waterhouse was no longer in the frame at Emmanuel for Lodge or Hall, and the College Order Book notes that it was agreed 'to consult Mr A. Blomfield for alteration and improvement of the Chapel and Lodge and Library'. Arthur Blomfield was probably introduced by Fenton Hort, elected Fellow of Emmanuel in 1872. Hort was formerly a Fellow of Trinity, where he and Blomfield had been contemporaries as undergraduates.[24]

From 1869 to 1876, Blomfield was involved in the refurnishing and redecoration of the Chapel at Trinity, which included painted decoration (now lost) and stained glass to a programme devised by the theologians Joseph Lightfoot and Brooke Westcott.[25] In 1872, Blomfield surveyed the Chapel at Emmanuel, which had been little changed since the altar painting was set up and the chandelier introduced in the 1730s. Blomfield, the son of a Bishop of London, had been in independent practice since 1856 and worked on several cathedrals. He was a champion of the gothic revival and in the 1870s was at work on the private chapel at Tyntesfield, one of the finest domestic chapels in the country, as well as restoring St Benet's in Cambridge.

He clearly found the classical Chapel at Emmanuel something of a challenge, with many 'glaring defects', although he recognised the significance of Wren. He wrote in a letter in June 1872:

> *After much consideration I have come to the conclusion that any great interference with the present architectural character of the chapel would involve more extensive alterations and consequently a larger outlay than I first anticipated … so much so indeed that if the character be altered it would be a serious question whether it would not be better to undertake the small additional outlay which would be required to build an entirely new one.*[26]

This dramatic suggestion may have been intended merely to provoke, but reminds us of changing attitudes and how many chapels were recast in the fashionable gothic revival style at this time so as to be better suited to the prevailing attitudes to liturgy. It is difficult to know how seriously this idea was entertained. Blomfield finished his point a bit more diplomatically: 'There are many reasons for preserving the present building if some of its more glaring defects can be remedied'.

To do this he proposed a raised altar, new choir seats and a cornice and frieze 'executed in painting'. Despite the fact he actively disapproved of the ceiling plasterwork, the College

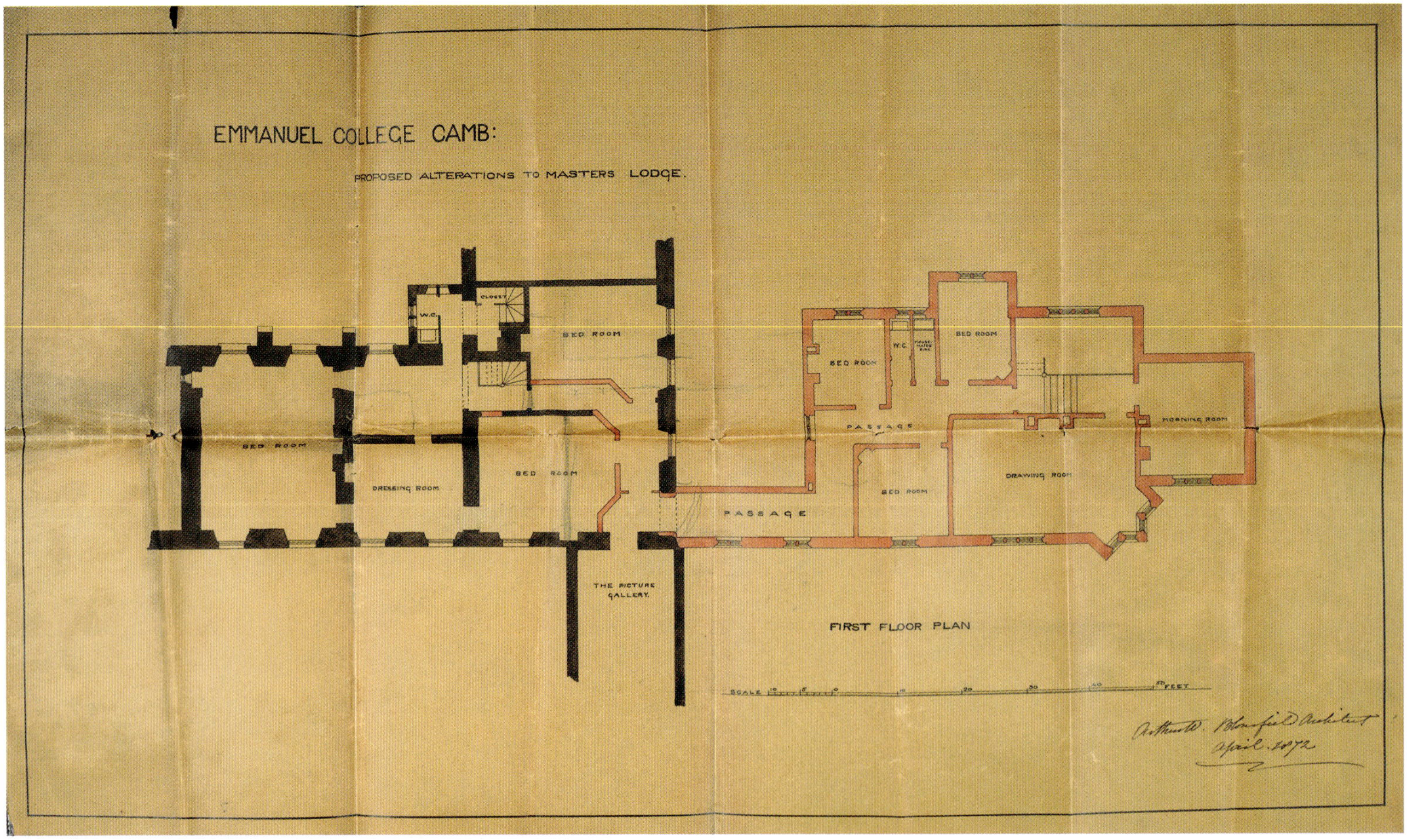

[above] *One of the proposals for the Master's Lodge by Arthur Blomfield, dated April 1872, not quite as executed. It shows a first-floor drawing room and morning room.*

[below, left & right] *The stately Master's Lodge designed by Blomfield, photographed shortly before its demolition in 1964; it follows the precedent set by George Gilbert Scott's Master's Lodge at St John's for a more free-standing residence.*

clearly guided him in June 1873 to 'give an alternative plan retaining the ceiling substantially as it is'.[27] Designs were supplied then for the College's consideration 'sufficiently complete to enable the College to form an opinion upon the probable effect of the changes as a whole', which were finally approved in June 1874. An appeal for subscriptions was issued on 10 October 1874, with the hope that they could remedy 'the blank and discoloured walls; the bare windows; the tasteless ornamentation and indifferent picture at the East end; the heavy and coarsely moulded plaster ceiling'.[28]

Blomfield's desire to replace the altar painting ('which I particularly dislike') with a 'reredos of marble or alabaster, with inlaid panels of mosaic' was not realised.[29] His designs for adding new windows into the east end and proposals for altering the plaster ceiling were also rejected. Heaton, Butler & Bayne were, however, commissioned to provide new stained glass for the existing windows in 1883.

Hort chose subjects for the windows illustrating the history of the English Church and the contribution of various members of Emmanuel (and several proto-Emmanuelites), and also provided names (of reformers and scholars) that were painted in the panels between the windows (covered over in 1927). In each window stand two figures against an early seventeenth-century pattern. They include early Church figures such as Origen and Augustine; reformers (in the broadest sense) such as John Colet, William Tyndale, John Fisher and Thomas Cranmer; and Emmanuel worthies Laurence Chaderton, William Bedell, Benjamin Whichcote, John Harvard, John Smith and William Law.[30]

Blomfield was also responsible for modifications to the late seventeenth-century Library, illustrated in a photograph published in Evelyn Shuckburgh's 1904 history of the College.[31] This Library was still then the privilege of the Fellows, so arrangements were made for the undergraduates to have a reading room on the ground floor of G staircase in Old Court. This was the beginning of a process that culminated in a new Library in the 1930s (see pp. 132–33), which was extended in the 1970s and again in 2009–11.[32] In 1876, Blomfield added a new oriel window (facing New Court) to the Parlour, enlarging the room and introducing more light.[33]

Blomfield built a neo-Jacobean Master's Lodge for Phear, for which he seems to have taken some of the advice that Waterhouse had given the Master. He built a new stately, gabled red-brick house reminiscent of a substantial rectory, which was designed to enjoy the south-western views over the Paddock and the pond.[34] Despite recent additions in the 1830s, the original Emmanuel Master's Lodge had always been considered 'inconvenient as a residence'.[35]

A late nineteenth-century Master was more likely to be married and to have a larger family and employ a greater number of servants than his predecessors, which meant that new lodges became a feature of Cambridge life. George Gilbert Scott's

The interior of the Chapel as altered by Blomfield with a raised altar and reredos, painted texts in the panels in between each window, and stained glass by Heaton, Butler & Bayne.

1860s' design for a free-standing Master's Lodge at St John's College may well have set a fresh standard.[36] Phear was a bachelor, but would have been acutely conscious of the necessary requirements for the dignity of the Mastership.

Blomfield's Master's Lodge required the demolition of a long thin range of buildings (seen in the survey of 1746 but not visible in Loggan's view published in 1690), thought to be early eighteenth-century in date, as well as a 'new Dining Room … erected at the Master's expence' as recently as 1835, and a 'new office and new entrance' of the same time, of which sadly there is no visual record.[37]

The new Lodge was generously provided with reception rooms, originally with a first-floor drawing room over the dining room (by 1911 the latter had became the drawing room, with a study above) occupying the north-eastern corner (close to the kitchen). The servants' quarters included a servants' hall beside the Cloister, and a narrow range running parallel to the then library, forming a small back yard with the kitchen.[38] Blomfield's building also required some reordering of the walls of the Fellows' Garden and new planting, although part of the garden was open to the Fellows' Garden and enjoyed views over the pond.

In 1884, Emmanuel celebrated its tercentenary with the installation of electric light, becoming the first college in Cambridge to begin to phase out gas lighting: a source of enormous pride to the science-minded Phear. It appeared not just in the Hall and Library but also in the Chapel, and would have dramatically changed the convenience and atmosphere of the College in winter months.[39]

The reforms stimulated by the Royal Commissions into the Universities of Oxford and Cambridge prompted discussions about affordable accommodation for undergraduates not drawn from the sons of landowners, wealthy industrialists and professionals. One solution was the provision of 'hostels', inspired partly by the early medieval pattern of accommodation at Cambridge.[40] At Emmanuel, the 1886 red-brick Hostel on the easterly edge of the Paddock was built to serve exactly this ideal. It had light sitting rooms or studies (described on the architect's plans as 'keeping rooms'), with intriguingly small single bedrooms screened by double doors; the Hostel had its own dining hall for breakfast.[41]

The Hostel was designed by William Fawcett, a Cambridge architect who had a solid (if unexciting) career, designing the Cavendish Laboratory and a number of boathouses and

The eastern edge of the Paddock is bounded by two red-brick Victorian buildings echoing the brick of Old Court: these are the Hostel, designed by William Fawcett and built in 1886, then extended in the mid-1890s by John Pearson, and Emmanuel House, also designed by Pearson, as a residence for the Senior Tutor, to the left of the picture.

restoring many important buildings, including the gatehouse of Queens' College.[42] The original plans and elevation show a utilitarian, upright building of three storeys with an attic storey above.[43] But Fawcett went to some trouble to base his design on the traditional college staircase pattern, and the detailing of the central doorcase was a careful visual echo of the doors of the 1630s' Old Court that the Hostel faces across the Paddock.

The Hostel as it is seen today has a rather more elegant character as a result of the additional wings both to the north and south, designed by John Pearson, an architect of considerable reputation. They date from 1893–94 and were added to provide yet more sets of rooms.[44] Pearson's ability to design well-judged picturesque buildings is also illustrated by his other Emmanuel commission: the carefully composed Emmanuel House, which he designed for the occupation of the Senior Tutor.

Pearson's wings, with their imaginative brickwork decoration and relief detail, and shaped dormers, both soften the utilitarian quality of Fawcett's original and also give the whole a more artistic neo-Queen Anne style, reminiscent of the 1870s–1880s' work of Basil Champneys at Newnham College. Pearson clearly wanted to 'lift' the overall feel of the building into something more fitting to its established garden setting.

Pearson's Emmanuel House is one of the more memorable architectural elements in the ensemble around the Paddock. It is a handsome red-brick building with stone dressings, loosely Jacobean in style (again with echoes of the 1630s' Old Court), of two principal storeys and an attic, and mullion-and-transom windows of stone, which were originally leaded. The main west-facing feature of the house is contrived into a three-storey bay window looking across the pond, giving a tower-like appearance, which Pearson grouped with a shaped gable.

The original 1885 designs for the Hostel by William Fawcett. The Hostel was intended to provide cheaper accommodation for undergraduates from less affluent backgrounds.

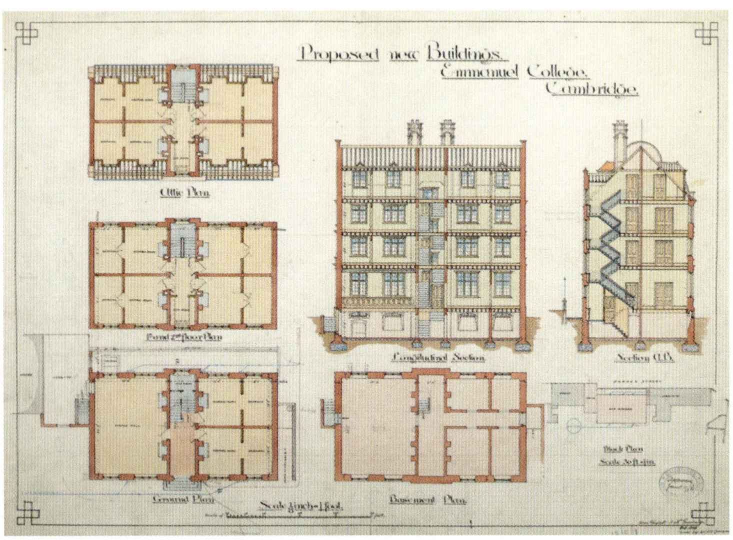

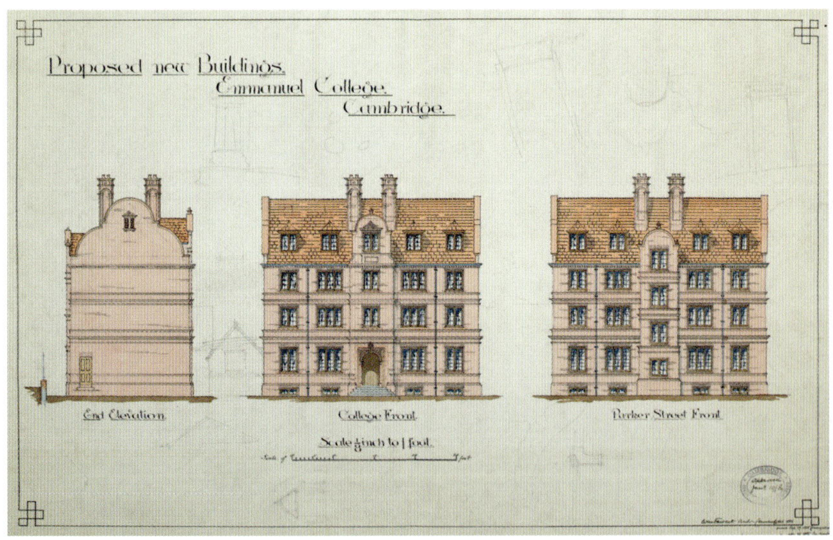

Old Emmanuel House, a sixteenth-century building used as Fellows' rooms refaced in the eighteenth century, which looked over the pond. The photograph was taken around 1890, after the completion of the Hostel but before the additions by Pearson and the demolition of Old Emmanuel House.

A distinguished gothic revival architect, Pearson is associated principally with churches and cathedral work (notably St Augustine's, Kilburn, of 1870, and Truro Cathedral, from 1878).[45] He had many country-house projects, and in the early 1890s was working on Number Two Temple Place, the handsome neo-Tudor estate office of the Astor family, overlooking the Embankment in London. In the early 1890s Pearson was also at work on the brick-and-stone Cloister Court at Sidney Sussex College; he had remodelled part of the west range of the Old Schools in the late 1880s.[46]

With the relaxation of the historic 'celibacy' condition, or rule against Fellows retaining their Fellowships on marriage (true for all Cambridge colleges), there was a concern that many of the rising generation of younger Fellows would find holding a College office irksome without residences.[47] The position of Senior Tutor was often occupied by men on the route to Masterships, and the provision of Emmanuel House, linked

[following pages, left] *Emmanuel House, built in 1894 to designs by Pearson, for the occupation of Emmanuel's Senior Tutor, who was more likely to be a married man after the relaxation of the traditional Cambridge rule, which meant that Fellows had to leave their College posts if they wished to marry.*

[following pages, right] *A detail of the 1890s' raised decorative brickwork of the additions made to the Hostel by Pearson, which transformed Fawcett's rather utilitarian design into something more in the neo-Queen Anne spirit.*

A view of Pearson's most famous work, Truro Cathedral in Cornwall.

Portrait of John L. Pearson (1817–1897) by Walter William Ouless (1848–1933).

to the existing Hostel and its new wings, may also have been intended to suggest a pastoral role over undergraduates resident in that building.

Emmanuel House has a curious sequence of entrances: a front door to the street, an entrance into the hall from the north side through a handsome loggia, and a third that suggests an entrance for undergraduates approaching the Senior Tutor's study. The first Senior Tutor to live in this building was William Napier Shaw. Emmanuel House ceased to be a residence in the 1930s, when its occupant, Thomas Shirley Hele, became Master and it was then divided it into sets of rooms for Fellows, as it mostly remains today.

Shaw was a keen oarsman and it was largely thanks to him that the College boathouse on the River Cam, designed by Marshall & Vickers, was built in 1896. It was extended in the 1990s by Thurlow, Carnell & Thornburrow, and preserves an admirably strong flavour of its Old English-style original.[48] The first College rowing crew is recorded in 1827 but the expanding undergraduate numbers under the Mastership of Phear led to an explosion of College sports clubs and societies, and the acquisition in the 1890s of a cricket and football ground off Adams Road, now bounded by Wilberforce Road. The pavilion and groundsman's cottage there were completed in 1910, to designs by Edward Ford Duncanson.[49] A racquets court, designed by Alan E. Munby, was built in the south-eastern corner of the Paddock in the early 1930s, replacing an earlier Eton Fives Court.[50]

The articles and clubs and society reports in the *College Magazine* reflect the richer, more communal, life of the undergraduate in the late nineteenth century. Other key early societies were the Debating Society, the Mildmay Essay Club and the Natural Science Club, founded in 1900 (renamed as the Thomas Young Club in 1929 and subsuming in 1953 the rival, and teasingly named, Natural Sciences Society that had been founded in 1910).[51] Increasing numbers also put demands on the College servants who, as was often the case in Cambridge colleges, were long-serving and long-suffering.

Family networks were a noted feature of Emmanuel staff. The College had four butlers from one family between 1786 and 1849; after that, William Edwards served for 30 years and William Townsend from 1899 to 1932. Head cooks were also long-lasting, with Thomas Wicks between 1807 and 1851, and George Tuck from 1874 to 1904.[52] Head porters were important figures and there was a complex hierarchy of assistant porters, gardeners, clerks, messengers, shoeblacks, bedders, laundresses and seamstresses.

A Cambridge bedmaker's role in the early twentieth century is described in *Backstairs Cambridge* (recalling the 'bedders' of Gonville and Caius College) and can serve to illustrate the life of an Emmanuel 'bedder' in the Victorian age:

> *Every morning every term, whatever the weather, Nellie and her mother tied on their large aprons and their ugly bonnets, took their*

Emmanuel College's boathouse on the River Cam, designed in a cheerful Old English style by Marshall & Vickers in 1896, and extended in the 1990s by Thurlow, Carnell & Thornburrow to either side in a similar character.

covered baskets and left their little terraced house near the railway station, to walk the mile into the centre of town and arrive at the college gate by six o'clock.[53]

Referring to the Cambridge requirement that bedders should be over a certain age and not too alluring to the undergraduate, it explains:

They may not have been beautiful but in order to keep their jobs they had to be punctual, honest and hard-working ... the first job of the morning was to rake out and carry away the ashes of the old fire, clean the grate and fill the coal scuttle with fresh coal.

Their duties were not light and the account continues:

coal buckets and, later, cans of hot water, had to be carried up three stories to the top rooms, while ashes and pails of dirty water had to be carried down again. It was their task to make beds once the students were up and to keep the rooms clean and tidy ... In the evening bedders walked all the way back to college again to 'turn down the beds'.

The 1888 Ordnance Survey showing the full extent of Emmanuel College at that time, and the enclosures of the Fellows' Garden and the Master's Garden after the creation of the new Master's Lodge by Blomfield.

The character of the College had been changed by the rise in the number of undergraduates and Emmanuel had perhaps recovered something of the zest of its early foundation. The city had changed too. So when Shuckburgh wrote his history of Emmanuel in 1904, he noted:

when the College was founded it was almost outside the town, with little or nothing between it and the open country: it was on the fringe of the University, remote from its heart and centre. Not only has the town grown round it but the University has crept up to it.[54]

Shuckburgh continued: 'The new Museums and laboratories on the site of the old botanic garden, and on the Downing ground opposite, have caused the College to be closer than most others to the crowded lecture rooms of the new learning.' It also made the pedimented entrance designed by Essex the focus of the 'head' of Downing Street, where it meets St Andrew's Street, with the domed lantern turret of Wren's Chapel sitting quirkily to one side.

In the College history of 1999, Christopher Brooke observed that Phear's long Mastership was 'over a generation which saw perhaps the most dramatic transformation of college and university life since the seventeenth century ... In Emmanuel, much new building was needed in the wake of the changes of this age.'[55] New accommodation and Lecture Rooms were built just before the First World War, becoming part of the unfolding twentieth-century story linked to a sequence of projects in the 1950s and 1960s, and the 1990s and early 2000s.

CHRIST'S COLLEGE
(Founded 1505)
On Site of
Gods House
(Founded 1446)
Second Court
First Court
Chapel
Master's Lodge
Hall
Kitchen
Larder
College Rooms
Lecture Room
Fields Court
Bradwell's Yard
Inland Revenue Office
Queens Arms (P.H.)
Drummer Street
Emmanuel Street
Bath
Fellows' Garden
Emmanuel House
College Rooms
Parker
St Andrew the Great
Great Pond
Master's Lodge
New Court
Chapel
Front Court
EMMANUEL COLLEGE
(Founded 1584)
On Site of
Dominican Friary
(Founded 1240)
Cloister
Hall
Kitchen
Buttery
College Rooms
Fish Pond
St Andrew's Ward
St Andrew's Street
St Andrew's Court
Bird Bolt Hotel (Temperance)
Downing Place
Balfour Laboratory
Castle Hotel
Sunday School
St Andrew's Street Chapel
(General Baptist)
(Seats for 500)
Spinning House
Smithy
Theatre Royal
Furness Lodge
Camden House
Park Terrace
Urinal

SAMUEL GEORGE PHEAR 1829–1918

In many ways a traditional bachelor don, Samuel Phear proved remarkable in his ability to manage the College during an important period of change.[56] He came from an academic family; his father held a Pembroke College living as rector of Earl Stonham, Suffolk, and had been a Fellow and tutor at Pembroke; his brothers were Cambridge Fellows and lawyers, with one occupying the role of Chief Justice of Ceylon.

Phear graduated from Cambridge in 1852 as fourth wrangler (a title denoting excellence among those awarded first-class honours in mathematics at Cambridge) and was made a Fellow of Emmanuel in 1853. In 1859 he was elected a Fellow of the Geological Society of London. In 1870 he was appointed to a parish in Loughborough, but the death of his fiancée sent him back into academia. After serving as Senior Tutor and Bursar, Phear was appointed Master in 1871, becoming a Doctor of Divinity the following year. He was Vice-Chancellor in 1874 and 1875.

Phear was noted for his scientific interests and was part of the Syndicate that led to the formation of the Cavendish Laboratory, which may explain why the Laboratory's architect, William Fawcett, was called in to design the Hostel. In June 1876, Phear made a payment on behalf of the Chancellor of £942 6s 0d to James Clerk Maxwell 'on account of apparatus and cases for your museum', as the Cavendish Laboratory was then described.[57]

During his time in charge, College government was radically overhauled and new statutes introduced after the two Royal Commissions. When he was elected Master, Emmanuel was one of the smallest colleges in terms of numbers of undergraduates; by his death, it had grown nearly threefold. As Christopher Brooke observes in the *History of the University of Cambridge*, the College became 'reasonably prosperous and exceptionally forward-looking'.[58] It was in a good state to face the challenges of the century ahead. The reform of which Phear was reputedly most proud was the introduction of electric light, 'a remarkable symbol of the coming of the new world'.[59]

SIR (FREDERICK) GOWLAND HOPKINS 1861–1947

One of the founders of modern biochemistry, Sir (Frederick) Gowland Hopkins ranks high among the distinguished scientists associated with Emmanuel College.[60] Born at Eastbourne, the son of a London bookseller, he attended the City of London School. After six months as an insurance clerk, he started on the path of a career chemist.

He took his degree in London and in 1888 went as a medical student to Guy's Hospital. After graduating, he taught physiology and toxicology at Guy's, and was put in charge of the Clinical Research Association's chemical department. In 1896, with H.W. Brook, he published influential discoveries on the halogen derivatives of proteins, followed by work on the crystallisation of blood albumins with S.N. Pinkus in 1898.[61]

In 1898, Hopkins married Jessie Anne Stevens – with whom he went on to have two daughters – and moved to Cambridge to work on the chemical aspects of physiology. Beginning with a lectureship, he became supervisor of Emmanuel's medical students and then a Fellow and a tutor. In 1910, he became a Fellow of Trinity College; he was elected an Honorary Fellow of Emmanuel in 1911 and maintained close connections with the College. He was elected to the Chair of Biochemistry in 1914, and in 1925 the department moved into the newly built Sir William Dunn Institute of Biochemistry.

Hopkins was knighted in 1925, and in 1929 received the Nobel Prize, jointly with Christiaan Eijkman, for his work on nutrition. He received the Order of Merit in 1935 and from 1930 to 1935 was President of the Royal Society. The work for which Hopkins is best known is his recognition of the importance, for nutrition, of substances present in small traces in natural fresh foods: namely 'vitamins'.[62]

[above] *Samuel Phear,* c.1890, *by Frederick Hollyer.*

[opposite] *Sir (Frederick) Gowland Hopkins, 1967, by Bernard Dunstan.*

CH_3.CHOH.CO

6

Out in the World

The twentieth- and twenty-first-century story of Emmanuel's buildings is a familiar one: pressure to provide more and more accommodation for undergraduates and postgraduates, and at the same time a concern, to protect the remarkable inheritance of the historic core of the College, expressing in stone and brick the continuity (and progress) of educational ideals and purposes.

The open Paddock has survived as mostly the same medieval enclosure acquired by Mildmay in the 1580s, while Front Court is hardly changed from the late eighteenth century. But progress has included one new large building within the Paddock, now the Library, and expansion of the site to the north and south, as well as the purchase of further hostel accommodation on Newmarket Road (Barnwell Hostel), Glisson Road (Blantyre House), 285–287 Hills Road and several houses close to Emmanuel in Warkworth Street, and the acquisition of Park Terrace in 1983. Within the historic site there have also been important later twentieth-century additions, including South Court in the 1960s and the Queen's Building in the 1990s.

This expansion of accommodation has been necessary because of the growth in College numbers. Emmanuel is today made up of a community of nearly 500 undergraduates, over 200 graduate students, as well as 90 Fellows and 150 members of staff covering the administration, care and servicing of a busy modern institution in a complex historic environment. Emmanuel ranks high academically, having consistently been in the top five colleges since 1998 and, on occasion, top of the 'league'.

The make-up of the College has altered, with an expanded Fellowship, an influx of graduate students, some post-doctoral researchers and, since 1976, women (the first female graduates arrived in 1976, a first Fellow in 1977 and undergraduates in 1979), but the long tradition of meritocratic entry has continued.[1] Co-education is the norm today, but is a major change from the long all-male history that preceded it. A late nineteenth-century time traveller might be struck by the familiarity of the scene, especially on a misty early morning before the twentieth-century [previous pages] *North Court, designed by Leonard Stokes to provide new accommodation, and completed in 1914 in an assured and original 'freestyle', drawing on late sixteenth-, seventeenth- and early eighteenth-century precedents.*

Portrait of Leonard Stokes (1858–1925) painted in 1912 by Sir William Orpen (1878–1931).

alterations become apparent, but Mildmay, descending from his time machine, would be puzzled by most of what he saw, and by the twinkling candles and sounds of a choir emerging from the east-orientated classical Chapel, as much as anything.

The building stock of Emmanuel's precinct has been considerably extended, usually at intervals of about 20 or 30 years, responding to different aspects of the status and needs of the College in a rapidly changing modern world. The expansion of University teaching and research in every area has its own impact, as does the modern emphasis on widening access and good results, leading to a growth in the importance of the Library (even in the age of knowledge in the electronic ether) and most recently in the additional significance of new technology in every area of life.

But Emmanuel remains an establishment devoted to the 'society' it serves, its buildings moulded to these needs and the support of academic activities, research, learning and technology. Important decisions are still taken by the Fellowship as a body, and a broad consensus must be achieved before major building projects are taken on. Further oversight is exercised by heritage bodies, the city council and Historic England.[2]

In fact, Emmanuel began the twentieth century with big plans in mind, to accommodate rising numbers and make it fit for the future. As Shuckburgh wrote in 1904,

> *the College is on the point of getting possession of Emmanuel Street in return for surrendering ground for a new street about 100 yards farther down St Andrew's Street, which – with the houses on the north side which are already in its possession – would enable it to erect almost as large a court as any in Cambridge.*[3]

This ambitious proposal had actually been agreed but in 1906 the town council (as it then was), with new plans of its own, recoiled and rejected the final agreement by 22 votes to 21. There was considerable embarrassment, and by way of compensation the council was persuaded to finance a linking tunnel under the road when further development of the College's land on the far side occurred.

Between 1906 and 1907, ideas for adding large buildings to enclose Chapman's Garden, and others in the Paddock, were explored, to provide more accommodation and lecture rooms: what Christopher Brooke called in 1999 a plan for 'not merely a hostel or group of hostels [but] ... an active centre of teaching'.[4]

In June 1907, Leonard Stokes was approached and was charged with realising some of this vision. An experienced and artistic architect who had designed many Roman Catholic churches and schools, Stokes belonged to what one critic called 'one of the great generations in the history of English architecture'.[5] He was, that same critic thought, to be grouped with 'Voysey, Prior, Lethaby, Ashbee, Ricardo and Baillie Scott'.[6] He had also only recently completed the Lincoln Grammar School for Boys, the design for which was exhibited at the Royal Academy in 1906.[7] In 1907, he was working on major additions to Downside School in Somerset.[8]

Endless discussion and debate went into the design of the only element to be added to the Paddock, a two-storey block to provide three lecture rooms and two classrooms: five teaching rooms in all. Hearing of the earlier exploratory designs, Stokes produced his own bold visions (see p. 134) for a new Library in Chapman's Garden and related residential buildings fanning out through the Paddock into the Fellows' Garden. One version would have realigned 'the great pond' to form part of a 'great court'. This would have doubled the accommodation of the College in a well-modulated series of courts but would have entirely dissipated the open leafy character the Paddock brings.

Stokes was gently but firmly advised by the Bursar, James Peace, that the building committee 'think you may take it as an instruction that no large plan of building on the Paddock or Fellows' Garden will be entertained by the Governing

[following pages] *The Library, designed by Leonard Stokes and opened in 1910 as Lecture Rooms, and extended to the east (left) when converted to a Library by Stokes's former assistant, George Drysdale, in 1930. The handmade bricks echo the bricks of Old Court, and the windows and ashlar the seventeenth-century buildings of the College; the gothic tracery is a nod to the ancient origins of the site.*

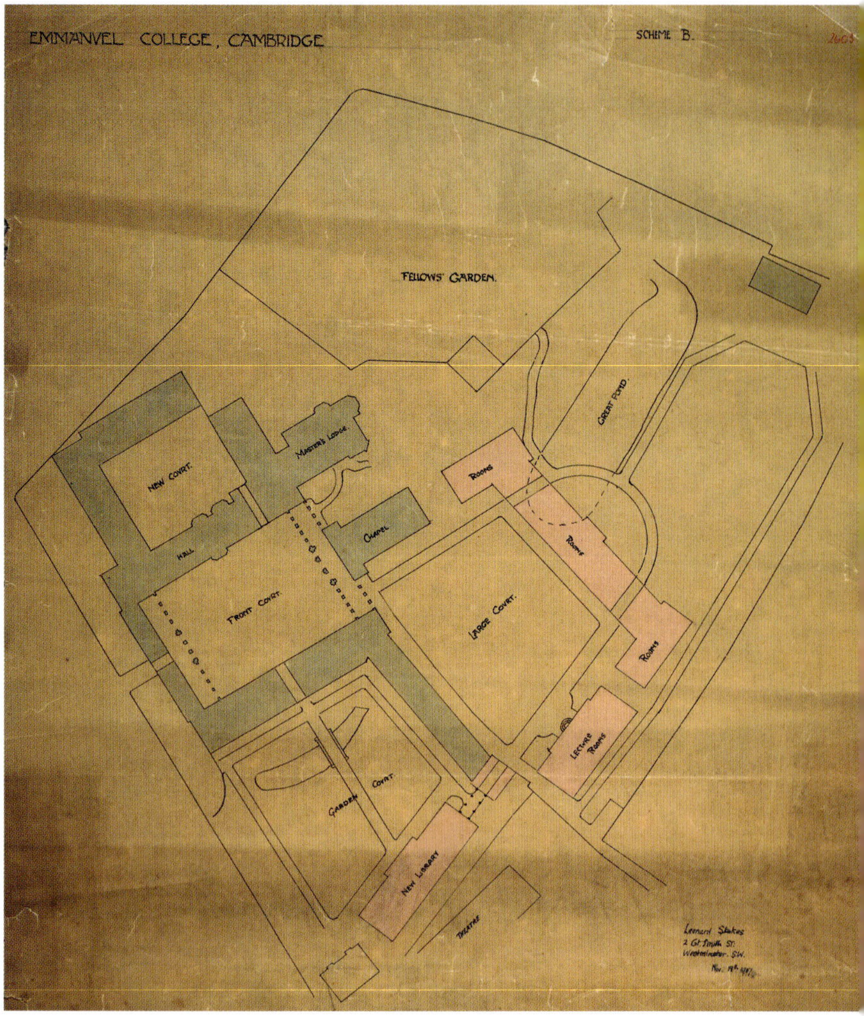

Stokes's suggestions made in November 1907 for new buildings within the old College boundaries, which would have sacrificed the gardenesque quality of the site.

Body of the present generation'; the park-like setting was thus preserved.[9] Stokes's tactful and artistic design for the Lecture Rooms (exhibited at the Royal Academy in 1908) was accepted after explorations of more classical and more gothic versions, and proved an original and subtle merging of the early and late seventeenth-century character, brick-and-stone, and mullion-and-transomed windows.[10]

After the tunnel had been agreed with the town council, Stokes was moved on to work on North Court, designed originally to be accommodation for 60 undergraduates and two Fellows, for which he presented a number of versions in 1909: one continued the brick-and-stone theme of the Lecture Rooms (which became the Library in 1930), with a tower and cloister where the tunnel arrived. The final version, completed in 1914, combined an early and late seventeenth-century style, around an L-shaped court.[11]

North Court is a reinforced concrete structure but faced in stone: Bath stone rubble and Weldon stone dressings. Much of the architectural character rests in the bold detail: the hooded doorways, Vanbrugh-like chimneys, elegant dormers and the overall sense of massing. A version of the design was also exhibited at the Royal Academy in 1910, and another (of the small cloister) in 1913.[12] As built, it has a strong echo of Stokes's 'freestyle' work at Minterne Magna, a new country house built for Lord Digby in 1904–6.[13] A Porters' Lodge was added and a small cloister to the western side.[14] The southern side of the court was originally open railings, but a stone wall was built in the 1960s and the small cloister converted into accommodation.

In 1927, the then Master of Emmanuel, Dr Peter Giles, spoke warmly of Stokes at a Royal Institute of British Architects discussion of a paper on the architect's work given by his assistant, George Drysdale. Giles recalled how 15 or 16 Fellows had followed up recommendations of different architects, and Stokes had been chosen even though 'the only thing he had done in Cambridge was a very small telephone exchange in a by-street'. The largest of the Lecture Rooms was considered 'by universal admission in the University … the finest lecture room in Cambridge'. The new court was 'one of the largest to be built

Stokes's presentation drawing of the 1909 proposal for North Court, in a brick-and-stone scheme closer in character to the design for the Lecture Rooms. This was one of the most ambitious new courts built in Cambridge since the early nineteenth century.

The detailing of the elevations of North Court has a distinctively baroque character, combined with Stokes's highly original celebration of texture and material.

in Cambridge for some centuries'. He added: '[Stokes] behaved extraordinarily well, considering how difficult it is to work for a body which is so large and has so many different interests to serve. The work was very well done'.[15]

North Court is certainly a handsome building and the sets of rooms were of a surprisingly generous provision, even by the standards of the day, consisting of a bedroom, sitting room and gyp room. But as the building was finished at the time the First World War was breaking out, North Court was immediately given over to the military when completed: army cadets from 1914 to 1919, and the Navy in 1919. As existing and potential undergraduates went to war, Emmanuel's numbers dropped and the new accommodation was not needed for students. Most admissions at this time consisted of overseas students, men medically unfit to fight and wounded ex-servicemen.[16]

Over 120 members of the College died in the First World War and they are remembered in the stone inscribed with their names in the Cloister. More elaborate plans were drawn up initially,

> *to erect at the south end of the Chapel Cloister an altar in stone, supporting a recumbent figure in front of the College Roll of Honour ... the recumbent figure is that of an officer, in uniform, with head reposing on a book, a shrapnel helmet at his feet ... to indicate life and immortality rather than repose and death.*[17]

When the memorial was unveiled it was a much simpler panel of names and dates, designed and executed by the same sculptor who had been approached for the first proposals, Ernest Gillick of Chelsea. The private notes of Governing Body meetings made

The newly completed North Court was handed over to military occupation in the First World War, and from 1914 to 1919 housed officer cadets attending short training courses.

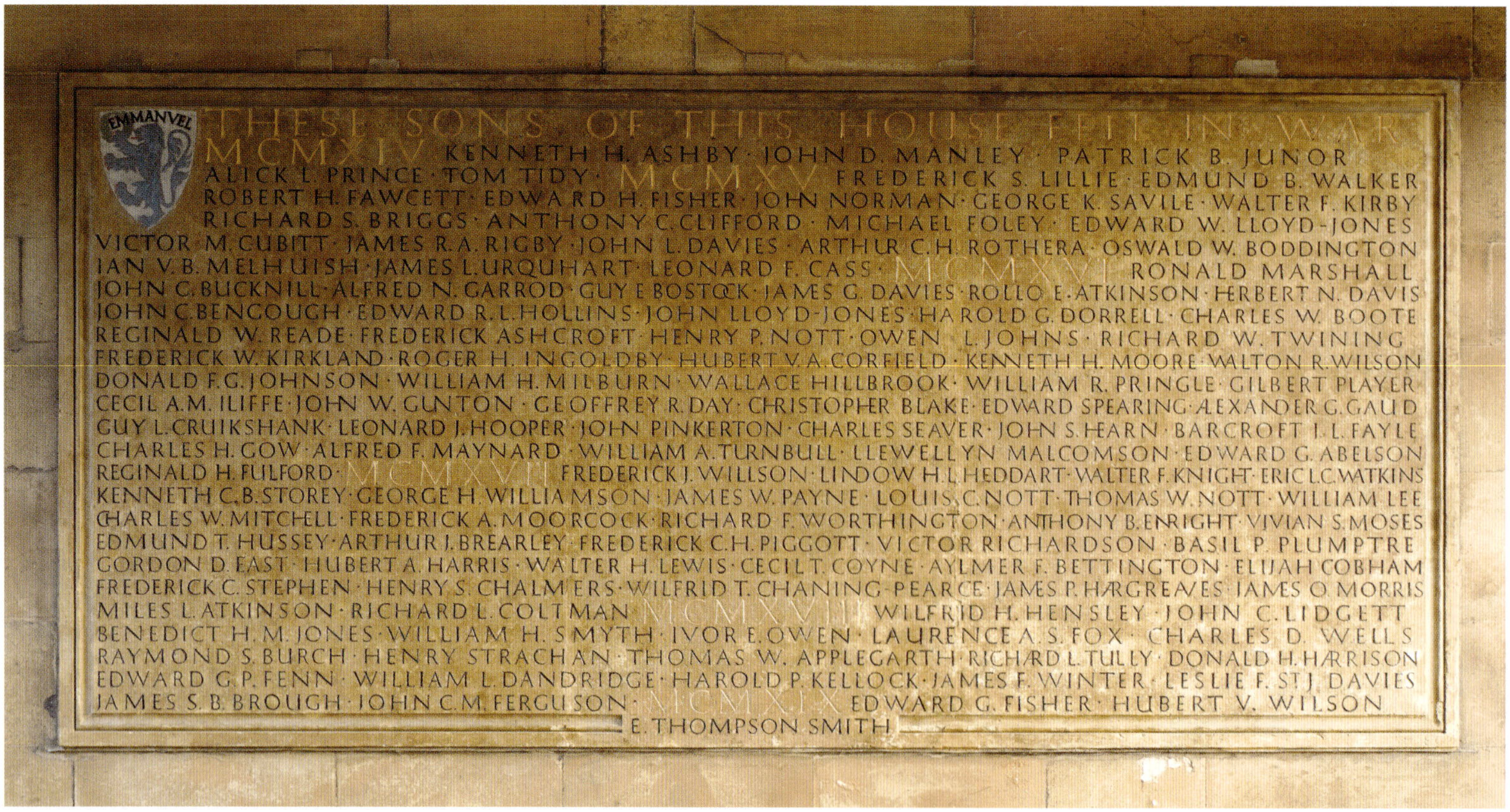

The simple memorial plaque to the Emmanuel College members who had died in the First World War, designed by the sculptor Ernest Gillick (1874–1951). An earlier scheme for a grand sculptural piece had been modified.

by Leonard Greenwood charted the delays and scaling down of the proposed memorial. In February 1921, the large scheme was rejected and there was a 'painful scene with Gillick', but modern eyes might well feel the reserve of the final result suitably dignified.[18]

The effect of the First World War on the economy of the University and colleges prompted another review of governance and finance, and new University statutes were drawn up in 1925. They set out a future of faculty-based teaching, so Emmanuel's Lecture Rooms were soon after converted into the Library, which also required the building to be extended to the east, in harmony with the original design. The work was given, in 1928, to Stokes's partner, George Drysdale, Stokes having died in 1925. It was completed in 1930.[19]

The main reading room still fills most of the first floor and has a tunnel-vaulted roof with plasterwork in the Wren manner. Drysdale also oversaw the removal of the books from the former Library (now known as the Old Library) and cleverly incorporated some of the early eighteenth-century bookcases. At the same time, he adapted the vacated Library to provide a second dining room to help with the expanding numbers of sittings for meals. This is now a reception room, hung with full-length portraits of former Masters, members and benefactors.

The first post-Second World War change was the demolition of the 1820s' Tudor-gothic-style kitchen wing in the mid-1950s, and its replacement by a copper-roofed new kitchen and an upper dining hall. This building was designed and executed by Robert Hurd, an Edinburgh-based architect and an Emmanuel graduate. Hurd was a leading conservation architect, credited with the successful rehabilitation of Canongate and other historic sites in Edinburgh.[20]

The driver behind the project was Edward Welbourne, Senior Tutor and later Master, who was an ambitious moderniser. He wrote in 1958 that the works were motivated by the need to increase 'the efficiency of our domestic life'. He liked Hurd and his assistant Ian Begg, and regarded the fact they were based far away as a good thing: 'It meant that we devoted proper time to

The main reading room of the Library, with its tunnel vault with 'Wrenaissance' plasterwork ceiling decoration. Some of the late seventeenth-century book presses were adapted for use in this room when it was converted from being the principal Lecture Room in 1930.

The Old Library (originally the Elizabethan Chapel) was adapted in 1930 to become a second dining hall, and is now used as a function room. The original timber screen of the 1580s' Chapel was revealed and restored by George Drysdale during these works, who removed the nineteenth-century timber ceiling installed by Blomfield.

the job, visiting responsibly, and not daring to leave the work to a subordinate'.[21] Knowing the new kitchen range to be especially visible from the public street, Welbourne said 'we wait for the sharp criticism, which will no doubt come'.[22]

Hurd's commission was a hard one, and with his conservation background he may well have preferred to adapt the existing building (he carefully preserved everything from the pre-nineteenth-century structure he was permitted, including a medieval arch, which he incorporated as one of the entrances to the kitchens). He was asked to provide a largely functional building, alongside a 1770s' elevation of some distinction on one side and a Tudor-gothic block on the other, all on a very public corner site.

Hurd's own self-consciously plain building, carefully lower than and set back from the main block (although marked out by its copper roof), provided a spacious and efficient open kitchen area with a large upper dining hall on the first floor, and other staff rooms and stores. The section nearest the Essex range is ashlared with tall, almost ecclesiastical windows that some have labelled as being in a modern 'Scottish vernacular' style. The more utilitarian northern section is rendered.

In the end, perhaps surprisingly, the greatest criticism came not from the conservationists, but from a group of younger design students, mostly from the Royal College of Art and other London architectural schools, who formed the self-confessed 'Anti-Ugly' or New Architecture Group. They came together in December 1958 especially to attack what they regarded as bland conservative design.[23]

The Anti-Uglies placed a coffin outside the Barclays Bank headquarters in Lombard Street, London, completed to a posthumous design by Herbert Baker, with the words 'Here lyeth British Architecture' and carried the same legend to Emmanuel. They organised a demonstration outside the College: another black-draped coffin appeared and additional banners saying 'Emmanuel's Cambridge Cowshed'.[24] According to *Varsity*,

[above] *Blomfield's Master's Lodge during demolition in 1964.*

[right] *The new Master's Lodge, designed by Tom Hancock and built in 1964: an austere split-level, brick-and-concrete structure.*

[left and above] *The reception rooms of the Master's Lodge are light and enjoy good views of the Chapel designed by Wren and the enclosed Master's Garden.*

they were supported by a good number of Emmanuel undergraduates, before repairing to the pub. But Nikolaus Pevsner observed that he 'thought it might be loved one day'.[25]

Hurd was very offended by the attack. The more bullish Welbourne brushed it off as a minor nuisance but he seems also to have felt emboldened to take a different approach to the College's late nineteenth-century Master's Lodge, which he personally disliked and was resolved to replace before he retired in 1964. Architect Tom Hancock (later well known as a town planner and theorist, who worked at Peterborough New Town and Canary Wharf) provided a design in 1963 and responded with a simplified, flat-roofed concrete structure faced in brown brick.[26] The split-level new replacement was partly built up on a garden platform created by the spoil from the older building.

Perhaps the best feature of the exterior of the very unadorned new Lodge (completed in 1964) was that it was pulled away from

[following pages] *The herb garden in New Court was designed by John Codrington and is a rare survival of an early 1960s' garden design. Codrington had been recommended to the College by Vita Sackville-West and also re-landscaped the Paddock, giving the pond its serpentine shape (using the brick and stone spoil from the Victorian Master's Lodge).*

the Chapel, Cloister and Old Library and revealed views of those older buildings. Internally Hancock created a surprisingly commodious house, with five bedrooms and a tall-ceilinged reception room on the raised ground floor. Lord St John of Fawsley, Master in the 1990s, also opened up the ground-floor rooms.[27]

Retired Fellows interviewed in 2015 could still recall how bricks and stones from the demolished Lodge were pushed in wheelbarrows into the Paddock and used to build up the new serpentine edges of the pond and to create the island. This was all part of a garden scheme proposed by John Codrington, who had been recommended to the College by Vita Sackville-West in 1960, initially to design the unusual herb-and-box-based planting of New Court.[28]

To increase student accommodation Emmanuel bought, and extended with the architects T.A. Bird and R.M. Tyler, a former nurses' hostel on Newmarket Road known as the Barnwell Hostel. This opened in 1962, the year the College bought and demolished the New Theatre Royal (1883–86) on the south-western boundary of the main site. The building – where Charlie Chaplin once performed and which hosted Cambridge Footlights between 1883 and 1936 (but which had become somewhat seedy by the 1960s) – had presented a towering blank wall to the College.[29] Some proposals for student accommodation were put forward by Hurd and Begg but not pursued. Instead, a new design was sought from Thomas Hancock, whose work on the Master's Lodge was then nearing completion.

This new court – South Court – was built in 1965–66 to create undergraduate rooms and some sets for Fellows.[30] Hancock's design was the largest modern redevelopment of the main site. The building, with two angled ranges of different lengths and three storeys (four storeys across the central section of the western part), was completed in 1966. These two concrete-framed ranges, faced in handmade brick and Clipsham stone, were linked in the middle by a spacious reception room and Junior Common Room complex, with a roof garden above, angled to make the most of light from the south.

These ranges provided 30 two-room sets, 40 bed-sitting rooms, four three-room flats for Fellows and two guest rooms. Hancock designed the accommodation around the top-lit staircases, built in cast-concrete sections. Large windows are framed by narrow bronze shutters to each side. Hancock also designed fitted furniture to give the undergraduates as much space and light as possible.[31] The impact of the building on Chapman's Garden was hardly subtle but a significant amount of accommodation was added to the College at one swoop.

South Court also had all 'mod cons' – running water and heating – rather in advance of Old Court, for which bathrooms and WCs were provided in South Court. New bathrooms and kitchens were tactfully inserted in 2015 in the garret floor of the seventeenth-century building. The first- and second-floor Fellows' rooms at the north end of South Court have some of the most attractive views of any in the College, with large plate windows looking down onto Chapman's Garden, trees, grass and the pond, and across to the brick south face of the Westmorland Building. This elevation, raised on piers and projecting into the garden, avoids the somewhat monolithic character of the rest of South Court.

It is interesting to contrast Hancock's buildings with the Queen's Building, designed by Michael and Patty Hopkins: a concert hall and lecture theatre completed in 1995, and a commission driven by the then Master, Lord St John of Fawsley (a legal academic, politician, former cabinet minister and chairman of the Royal Fine Art Commission). Michael Hopkins had worked briefly in Hancock's office in the mid-1960s before working with Norman Foster and then founding

The proposal for South Court, designed by Tom Hancock to provide further accommodation and some sets for Fellows. It was mostly built over the site of the late nineteenth-century New Theatre Royal and the garden of 55 St Andrew's Street.

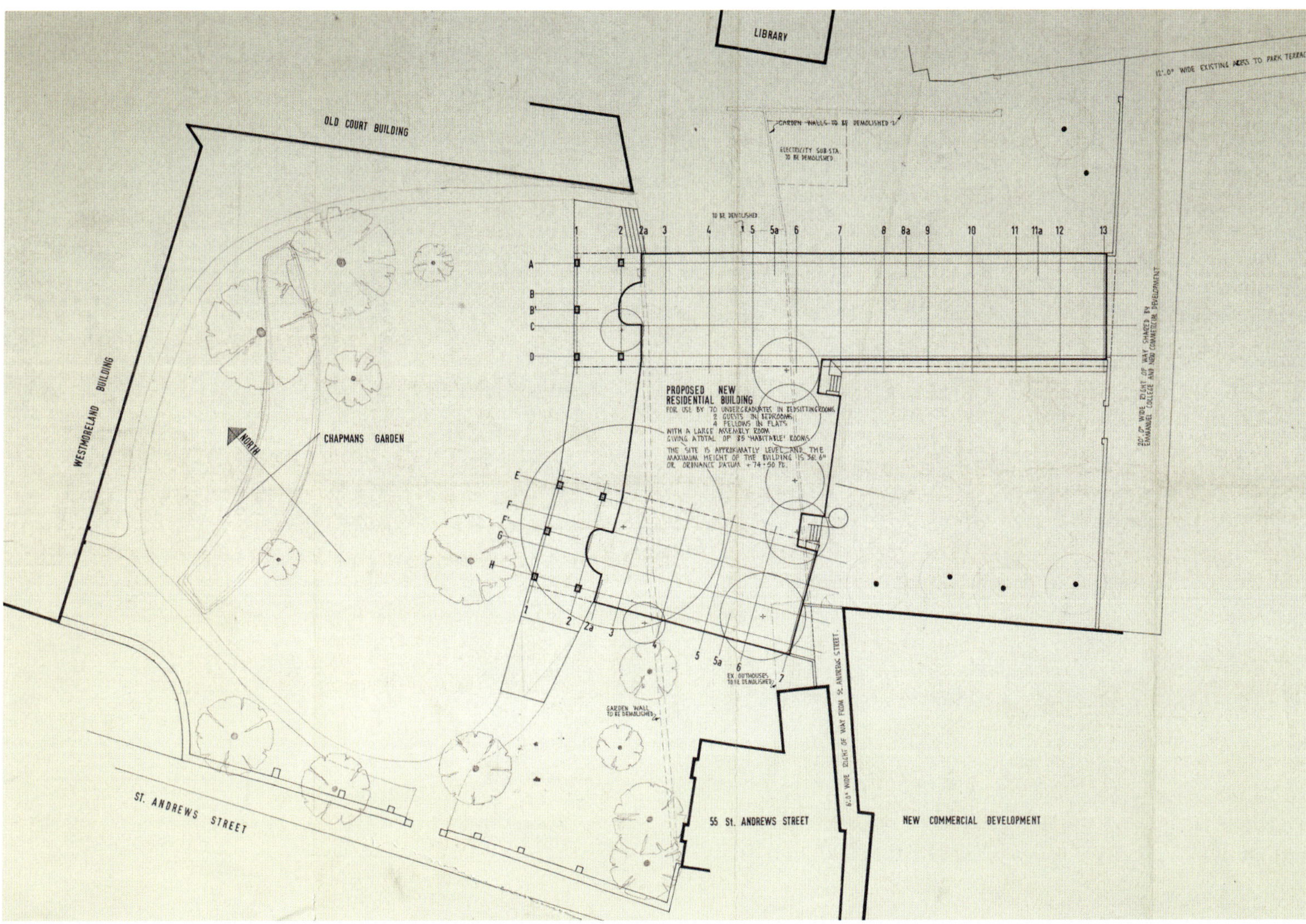

[left] *South Court facing Chapman's Garden, with Fellows' rooms looking over the garden, and the Junior Common Room complex linking the two angled ranges. It is faced with brick and Clipsham stone.*

[right] *Three presentation sketches by Tom Hancock for the interior treatment of the different room sets in South Court, with fitted furniture and a window seat over the services.*

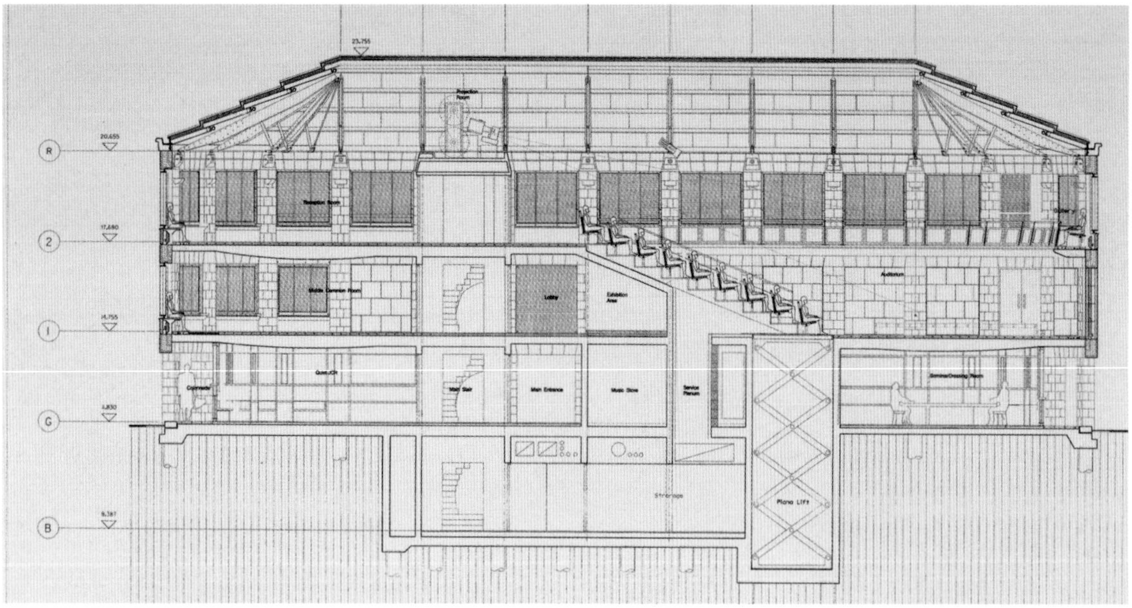

A longitudinal cross-section of the Queen's Building showing the structure and the volume of the theatre space.

his own practice with his wife, Patty, in 1976. They quickly built an international reputation in the 1980s for technologically adventurous buildings, including the Schlumberger Institute in Cambridge and the Mound Stand at Lord's Cricket Ground; in 1994 Michael and Patty Hopkins jointly received the Royal Institute for British Architects' Gold Medal.[32]

The Queen's Building was designed to be one of Cambridge's only freestanding engineered stone structures of the twentieth century, with engineers Buro Happold, closely advised by Professor Chris Burgoyne, engineering Fellow of Emmanuel.

A round-ended oblong structure of three storeys, the Ketton limestone in which the Queen's Building is constructed is from the same quarry as the stone that was used for the Chapel. Sir Michael recalls how they devised the curved end to help fit a large building into a tight site, and how their design for Emmanuel was informed by their new opera theatre at Glyndebourne.[33] There is a detached glass stair tower, and a narrow cloister-like passage runs round the ground floor echoing the 1670s' Cloister by Wren. The whole has a compact grandeur that speaks well to its historic context. The building is finely crafted, with interiors lined with American oak. Several modest garages were removed and the arches of the Stokes-designed arcade linking to the tunnel restored.

In addition to its aesthetic elegance, in engineering terms the Queen's Building is unique.[34] The stone is load-bearing and to avoid cracking (given the oval ends) it is also 'post-tensioned' by stainless-steel rods within the uprights. This creates a stone frame, and the stone panels and windows are all flush with the surface. Professor Burgoyne observed:

> *The significance of the Queen's Building is that it is an 'Engineered Stone Building'; in which the stone is performing the role that would normally be undertaken by a steel or concrete frame, allowing much bigger windows and a much reduced area of stone than would be typical of a conventional masonry building.*

Michael and Patty Hopkins who designed the Queen's Building, a new lecture and concert hall, with music practice and meeting rooms.

[opposite] *The elegant glazed separate staircase to the south-east of the Queen's Building.*

Two views of the interior of the Queen's Building auditorium with its finely detailed American oak fittings.

The Queen's Building, opened in 1995 by HM Queen Elizabeth II, is one of the finest buildings of late twentieth-century Cambridge, combining respect for the traditional context with structural ambition and innovation. It is built in Ketton limestone, the same stone that was used for Wren's Chapel.

THIS FOUNDATION STONE
WAS LAID BY
HER ROYAL HIGHNESS
THE PRINCESS OF WALES
IN THE YEAR OF OUR LORD 1993
ON THURSDAY NOVEMBER 11
LORD ST JOHN OF FAWSLEY
BEING MASTER

The Graham Watson Room in the Library containing a collection of colour-plate books, presented by Emmanuel member Graham Watson in 1975, along with the bookcases in which they are kept.

Hopkins Architects has since worked at Princeton and Rice Universities, and is currently working on a new building at Harvard (the Richard A. and Susan F. Smith Campus Center): a happy link to the longer history of Emmanuel.[35]

New buildings continue to be added and accommodation ranges built along the edges of the site. In the 1980s, additions were made at the south-eastern corner by Nicholas Hare Associates; the practice also remodelled the interior of the current Porters' Lodge with its handsome sliding oak-glazed screens and counter. Further accommodation has been provided in the terracotta-clad New South Court and pale brick New Cloister block off North Court, both from the design department of Bidwells.[36] Stokes's North Court itself has just been refitted (2009–16) to provide more comfort, privacy and security for the modern student, within the stately Edwardian original.

The 2009–11 Kilburn Nightingale Library extension wraps round a 1974 Library extension, creating a dramatic vertical rhythm and providing new study spaces around the stacks.

Perhaps the most dramatic recent addition is the Library extension by Kilburn Nightingale, completed in 2011, a remodelling of the rather more stark and practical extension of 1974 by Arthur Gibbon and Michael Driver of Cruickshank & Seward, and creating a new entrance.[37] The employment of timber, the vivid vertical lines of colour and the provision of extra work spaces for undergraduates make use of a different aspect of the College.

Some students and Fellows now normally approach the College from the southern gates. This is a result of the College's 1983 purchase (from Jesus College) of the fine 1830s' neo-classical Park Terrace facing Parker's Piece, designed by Charles Humfrey (see p. 108). The acquisition, under the Mastership of Derek Brewer, was considered a fitting celebration of the College's quatercentenary. Park Terrace has considerably added to the stock of accommodation, and about 25 per cent again to the central site, with its domestic gardens, and interesting ranges of outbuildings and former haylofts. It has also created a fresh face to the outside world: another new horizon.[38]

One of the modern projects that vividly illustrates changing attitudes to inherited buildings is the restoration of the College Chapel in 2004, by conservation architect Peter Inskip, who carefully reinstated the architectural arrangement of the Chapel as completed in the 1680s, while retaining its 1730s' amendments for the altar painting and chandelier.[39] The principal alterations were the return of the 1687 reredos to its original position, the restoration of its gilding, inscriptions and the plaster frame above, as well as the refixing of the altar rails to their late seventeenth-century position. Nineteenth-century prayer desks had already been removed in the 1990s; now the marble pavement was extended to fill the spaces between the original collegiate seating. It often comes as a surprise when this new work is pointed out to visitors, so well does the result sit in the whole. This project, well researched and tactful, represents both the renewed reputation of Wren in the twentieth century and modern ideals of preserving the best of the past for future generations.

Emmanuel still has the Paddock at its heart and this is as defining a feature of the College as its classical Front Court.[40] The tree planting begun by Chaderton has continued, and the gardens are maintained to a high standard with care and devotion by head gardener, Christoph Keate, and his team. Mature trees are still in abundance in the Paddock, Fellows' Garden and Chapman's Garden.[41]

Few visitors will fail to be impressed by the sweeping canopy of the great oriental plane (*Platanus orientalis*) in the Fellows' Garden, planted in the early 1800s. More colour contrast and flowering trees were introduced in the 1960s by the designer John Codrington, who created the herb garden in New Court, with its diagonal lines and segmental beds, today considered a rare survival of 1950s–1960s' garden design.[42]

The trees at Emmanuel are an important part of the overall ensemble and almost indivisible from the architectural experience of the buildings. In the summer they virtually meld together. A certain self-conscious wit has gone into some of the post-war tree-planting: the island in the Paddock's pond is crowned with a Swamp cypress (*Taxodium distichum*), while the Caucasian wingnut tree (*Pterocarya fraxinifolia*) nearby stands in memory of a Fellow who was Professor of Aeronautical Engineering, Sir Bennett Melvill Jones.[43]

The *Metasequoia* in Chapman's Garden was planted after the Second World War, a type known only in fossils until rediscovered by botanists in a remote part of China (and hence known as 'the Fossil Tree', *Metasequoia glyptostroboides*).[44] It might be taken as a symbol of the cycle of ages, of loss, rediscovery and survival – and new futures. Emmanuel has always built on its past. It has reinhabited and reinvented inherited structures for new worlds, material and immaterial. These layered buildings, old and modern – and the gardens that surround them – are in their turn continually being filled with new people and fresh life.

The Fellows' Garden looking south: an oasis of calm in what has become the city centre.

[following pages] *Planted in the early 1800s, the famous oriental plane (*Platanus orientalis*) in the Fellows' Garden is a memorable and admired feature of Emmanuel College's highly cherished grounds.*

EDWARD WELBOURNE 1894–1966

Edward Welbourne was brought up in Lincolnshire, the son of a police officer. He came to Emmanuel in 1912 as a scholar from De Aston grammar school in Lincolnshire, and wrote later of his social and intellectual milieu at the College 'from the careful middle class, parsons' sons, widows' sons'. He shared with them the experience of watching his pennies and eating frugal meals, but also the independence and stimulating discourse of College life.[45]

Welbourne took a double first in history and rowed for the College, before serving, and being wounded, in the First World War, during which he was awarded the Military Cross. An economic historian, famous 'talker' and inspired (if sometimes maverick) lecturer, his early study of the miners' unions won several awards. He was not much published, committing his energies to lectures and tutorials.[46]

Master of Emmanuel for 13 years, Welbourne wanted to help change and refresh the College, and in the late 1950s and 1960s he made it a 'time of much repair and rebuilding'. He oversaw the new kitchens and upper dining hall, and the complex planning and fundraising for South Court, which provided much-needed undergraduate accommodation and Fellows' sets looking over Chapman's Garden. He was also a driving force in the replacement of the 1870s' Master's Lodge, which was pulled down and replaced with the more compact 1965 building.

A legendary figure at Emmanuel, Welbourne was, above all, a committed College man. He rose from undergraduate to Fellow, Tutor, supervisor in history, Senior Tutor and Master, and was influential as admissions tutor, conducting many interviews personally and shaping the make-up of the College. Frank Stubbings wrote in 1983: 'His concern for the College was always primarily in terms of people. As admissions tutor he had a flair for spotting the promising boy. If he occasionally acted without the Fellows' knowledge, he said, it was not without their consent.'[47]

[left] *Edward Welbourne, 1958, by Ernest Hayes.*

[opposite left] *Ronald Norrish, 1968–69, by William Evans.*

[opposite right] *George Porter (Lord Porter of Luddenham), 1994, by Susan Ryder.*

There can be no greater recognition of the importance of scientific achievement in the twentieth-century College than the 1967 Nobel Prize, awarded jointly to Ronald Norrish, Fellow of Emmanuel, and George Porter, a former Fellow, 'for their studies of extremely fast chemical reactions, effected by disturbing the equilibrium by means of very short pulses of energy'.[48]

Norrish had been Porter's supervisor. He served with the Royal Artillery in the First World War and was taken prisoner, before going up to Emmanuel in 1919 and taking a double first in natural sciences. A Research Fellow from 1925, he became Professor of Physical Chemistry in 1937, overseeing an expansion of the chemistry department and its move to laboratories on Lensfield Road.[49]

George Porter was educated at Thorne Grammar School and, in 1938, went as Ackroyd Scholar to Leeds University. In the Second World War he was an officer in the Royal Naval Volunteer Reserve Special Branch, concerned with radar.[50] Early in 1945, he went to Cambridge to work as a postgraduate research student with Norrish. He studied, by flow techniques, the free radicals produced in gaseous photochemical reactions, and developed the idea of using short pulses of light, of shorter duration than the lifetime of the free radicals. He began the construction of an apparatus for this purpose in the summer of 1947. Together with Norrish, he applied this to the study of gaseous free radicals and to combustion.

In 1955, Porter went to the University of Sheffield as Professor of Physical Chemistry. He was Director and Fullerian Professor of Chemistry at the Royal Institution and the Director of the Davy Faraday Research Laboratory. He became a Fellow of Emmanuel in 1952 and an Honorary Fellow in 1967. He was elected a Fellow of the Royal Society in 1960 and awarded the Davy Medal in 1971, becoming a peer in 1990.

[following pages] *The 1670s' Gallery set for the dessert course for a special dinner, part of the long Cambridge dining tradition that encourages conversation and exchange of views between members and guests, students and Fellows from many disciplines.*

Notes

INTRODUCTION · PAGES 13–21

1. The most comprehensive and up-to-date account of College history, the people and intellectual traditions and the wider College estates is Sarah Bendall, Christopher Brooke and Patrick Collinson's *A History of Emmanuel College, Cambridge* (1999), which has been an enormous help, as has Dr Bendall herself with guidance and advice, and Amanda Goode, College Archivist, who has been generous with time and support. The account of the College in Robert Willis and John Willis Clark, *The Architectural History of the University of Cambridge and of the Colleges of Cambridge* (1886), vol. II, pp. 687–722, has been an important source, as has the Royal Commission on the Historical Monuments of England (RCHME), City of Cambridge volume, Parts I and II (1959).
2. See http://hansard.millbanksystems.com/commons/1943/oct/28/house-of-commons-rebuilding (accessed 25 July 2016).
3. Stubbings 1989–90, vol. lxxii, p. 29.
4. The gardens and trees are explained in detail in Sealy and Gray 1996.

CHAPTER I · PAGES 23–29

1. Salzman (ed.) 1948, vol. II, pp. 269–76; RCHME 1959, Part I, p. lxx.
2. Zutshi (ed.) 1988, 'The Cambridge Dominicans', introduction by Robert Ombres, OP, pp. I–2.
3. Ibid., p. I; Zutshi and Ombres 1990, pp. 313–73; C.R. Palmer, 'The friar-preachers, or Blackfriars, of Cambridge', *The Reliquary, Quarterly Archaeological Journal and Review* (July 1863–October 1894); vol. 25 (January 1885), pp. 137–42, 206–11, gives extensive references to the Dominicans from the Public Record Office; I am grateful to Dr Donal Cooper for this reference and helpful advice.
4. Salzman (ed.) 1948, vol. II, pp. 269–70.
5. Bendall et al. 1999, p. 7.
6. Salzman (ed.) 1948, vol. II, p. 271.
7. Willis and Clark 1886, vol. III, pp. 578–88.
8. Willis and Clark 1886, vol. II, p. 694; and Bendall et al. 1999, pp. 7–10.
9. Stubbings 1969, pp. 94–104, includes useful reconstructions of the arched windows of the north wall and placing of buttresses, especially p. 98; Schenluhn 2000, pp. 146–47, illustrates comparative mendicant church plans and shows the Cambridge church to have been on the narrow side.
10. Bendall et al. 1999, p. II.
11. Alison Dickens, 'Archaeological excavations in the Master's Lodge', Report No. 110.
12. Salzman (ed.) 1948, vol. II, p. 272.
13. Bendall et al. 1999, pp. 8–10.
14. Ibid., p.10; and https://oxfordfriars.wordpress.ncsu.edu/history (accessed 8 November 2016).
15. Salzman (ed.) 1948, vol. II, p.269.
16. Ibid.
17. Ibid., citing E.S. Roberts (ed.), *The Works of John Caius, M.D.* (Cambridge, 1912), pp. 40–41.
18. Salzman (ed.) 1948, vol. II, p. 270.
19. Ibid.
20. Bendall et al. 1999, p. II; https://plato.stanford.edu/entries/holkot (accessed 29 December 2016).
21. Gumbley 1938, p. 21.
22. Bendall et al. 1999, p. 9. Christopher Norton, David Park and Paul Binski, *Dominican Painting in East Anglia: the Thornham Parva Retable and the Musée de Cluny Frontal* (Woodbridge, 1987), pp. 88–91, suggests the priory at Thetford. Pamela Tudor-Craig suggests the Cambridge Black Friars in her review of the same in the *Antiquaries Journal*, vol. 68 (1988), pp. 367–68. Ann Massing (ed.), *Painting and Practice: the Thornham Parva Retable: Technique, Conservation and Context of an English Medieval Painting* (Cambridge and London, 2003), pp. 9–14, argues that it was probably produced in Norwich. Most recently, Norwich has been suggested by Nicholas Rogers (see Rogers 2010, pp. 185–93).
23. Gumbley 1938, p. 8; and Zutshi and Ombres 1990, pp. 332–33, 338–41.
24. Philip Wilkins, *Our Lady and English Martyrs Cambridge* (Cambridge, 1965), pp. 44–46.
25. Ibid., p. 45. However, Elizabeth Smale, 'Dominican art and architecture in the Cambridge visitation, *c.*1220–*c.*1540', PhD thesis (University of Cambridge, 2002) notes that the most recent analysis by style suggests that the figure currently in the Church of Our Lady is sixteenth- or even seventeenth-century Low Countries work.
26. Salzman (ed.) 1948, vol. II, pp. 274–75.
27. Ibid.
28. Ibid.
29. Ibid., p. 275, mentions sales of materials to the churchwardens of Great St Mary's, Cambridge; Willis and Clark 1886, vol. II, p. 688.
30. Willis and Clark 1886, vol. II, p. 688.
31. Ibid.
32. Emmanuel College Archive (ECA): Deeds Box I, EII.
33. Bendall et al. 1999, p. 12.
34. Jones 2015, p. 87.
35. Lehmberg 1964, p. 115.

CHAPTER 2 · PAGES 31–53

1. Shuckburgh 1904, p. 23.
2. ECA: Deeds Box I, EII.
3. Baggs 2002, plate I.
4. Shuckburgh 1884, p. 7.
5. Shuckburgh 1904, pp. 5–7.

Detail of ashlar in Front Court.

6. Lehmberg 1964, p. 229.
7. Information from Amanda Goode, Archivist, based on the Admissions Register, November 1584 to December 1586: ECA: CHA.1.4C.
8. Pevsner and Bradley 2014, pp. 196, 223–24.
9. Foyle 2016.
10. Shuckburgh 1904, p. 5.
11. Stubbings 2005, p. 65.
12. ECA: COL.9.10.1: letter from Sir Thomas Legge to Sir Walter Mildmay; and see Lehmberg 1964, p. 23.
13. ECA: Deeds Box 1, D5.
14. Bendall et al. 1999, p. 43; and Blomefield 1751, p. 116.
15. Stubbings 1983, p. 4.
16. Bodleian Libraries, University of Oxford: Cambridge Map, John Hamond's map of Cambridge, 1592.
17. Twigg 1986, p. 23.
18. Willis and Clark 1886, vol. II, p. 695.
19. ECA: COL.9.10.1; Lehmberg 1964, p. 230.
20. Collinson, 'Chaderton, Laurence (1536?–1640)', *ODNB*, 2004.
21. Shuckburgh 1884, p. 9, n. 2, £150 supplied for a dwelling for Chaderton by Sir Henry Killigrew.
22. ECA: Plans/Gen.1; and Bendall et al. 1999, p. 32.
23. Rupp 1984, pp. 24–27, 26.
24. Collinson, 'Chaderton, Laurence (1536?–1640)', *ODNB*, 2004.
25. Fuller 1840, p. 278.
26. Stubbings 2005.
27. Ibid., pp. 25–26.
28. Bendall et al. 1999, p. 24.
29. Stubbings 2005, p. 95.
30. Ibid.
31. Brewer 1984, pp. 43–46, 44; and see pp. 77–81, 77.
32. ECA: CHA.1.4.A.
33. Ibid.
34. David Adshead and David Taylor (eds), *Hardwick Hall: a Great Old Castle of Romance* (New Haven and London, 2016), p. 28.
35. Willis and Clark 1886, vol. II, pp. 700–1.
36. Stubbings 1977, p. 3.
37. Collinson, 'Chaderton, Laurence (1536?–1640)', *ODNB*, 2004; this is the age given on his memorial in the College Chapel.
38. Shuckburgh 1889, pp. 9–19, 18.
39. Bendall et al. 1999, p. 49.
40. Ibid., p. 64.
41. Ibid., pp. 228–29.
42. Winthrop 1864, vol. 1, pp. 309–11.
43. Bendall et al. 1999, p. 233.
44. Ibid., p. 234 (Thomas Shepherd, a fellow passenger).
45. Ibid., p. 237.
46. Ibid., p. 238.
47. Willis and Clark 1886, vol. II, pp. 697–98.
48. Ibid.
49. Shuckburgh 1904, p. 9.
50. Sarah Hutton, 'The Cambridge Platonists', *The Stanford Encyclopedia of Philosophy* (Winter 2013 edition), Edward N. Zalta (ed.), http://plato.stanford.edu/archives/win2013/entries/cambridge-platonists (accessed 25 July 2016).
51. Bendall et al. 1999, pp. 240–45.
52. Ibid., p. 246.
53. Ibid.
54. Ibid., p. 247.
55. Ibid., p. 252.
56. Stubbings 1977, p. 6.
57. Ford, 'Mildmay, Sir Walter (1520/21–1589)', *ODNB*, 2004.
58. Ibid.
59. Lehmberg 1964, p. 14.
60. Ibid., p. 48.
61. Stubbings 1977, p. 6.
62. Wright, 'Frankland, Joyce (1531–1587)', *ODNB*, 2004; Bendall et al. 1999, p. 105.
63. Ibid.
64. Bendall et al. 1999, p. 41.
65. Ibid.; Stubbings 1983, no. 3.
66. Shuckburgh 1884, pp. 13–14.
67. Collinson, 'Chaderton, Laurence (1536?–1640)', *ODNB*, 2004.

CHAPTER 3 · PAGES 55–81

1. Bendall et al. 1999, p. 256.
2. Ibid., pp. 269–70.
3. Ibid., p. 268.
4. Ibid., p. 265.
5. Ibid.
6. Ibid., p. 267.
7. ECA: COL.9.10.16: William Sancroft letter to Ezekiel Wright, 17 June 1663, verso.
8. Bolton and Hendry (eds) 1936, vol. XIII, pp. 51–55, and Musson, forthcoming 2017.
9. Thanks to Helen Carron, College Librarian Emmanuel, for this information; a catalogue is in progress.
10. Tatton-Brown 2000, pp. 79–80.
11. Jardine 2002, pp. 229, 257, 287–88.
12. Grimstone 2009, p. 9.
13. I am grateful to Professor John Adamson for this interesting suggestion.
14. Pevsner and Bradley 2014, pp. 165–66.
15. Ibid., p. 165: Wren's building was Cambridge's 'earliest purely classical building'. For the affirmation of the Restoration and the contribution of Pearce, see Grimstone 2009, pp. 12–13, 20, 113–19.
16. Grimstone 2009, pp. 113–16, where he suggests Edward Pearce might have also contributed to the design of Emmanuel.
17. For the importance and context of the Sheldonian, see Geraghty 2013.
18. Ibid., pp. 66–69.
19. Fürst 1956, p. 5; Whinney 1970, pp. 40–41.
20. Downes 1982, p. 45.
21. Colvin 2008, p. 1159.
22. Ibid., p. 1158.
23. For Holdsworth's legacy, see Bendall et al. 1999, pp. 270–71.
24. Willis and Clark 1886, vol. 1, p. 718.
25. Souden 1984, pp. 56–60, 58.
26. Bendall et al. 1999, p. 273. The total cost of the Chapel was £3,972, and Sancroft contributed £600 himself.
27. Stubbings, 1977, p. 11.
28. http://www.british-history.ac.uk/survey-london/vols29-30/pt1/pp. 31-55#anchorn175 (accessed 29 December 2016).
29. Geraghty 2007, cat. no. 8, p. 24.
30. Seckler 1954, p. 43.
31. ECA: CHA.1.1.1, 1668, p. 1 of the disbursements by Dr Bright; 'portico gallery' on p. 1 in the same accounts.
32. Bendall et al. 1999, pp. 272–73.
33. Stubbings 1977, p. 9.
34. Willis and Clark 1886, vol.1, p. 706.
35. Jardine 2002, p. 229.
36. ECA: CHA.1.1.1, 1668, p. 8 of the disbursements by Dr Bright, payment for Mr Wren's coach to London, as discovered by Johanna Heinrichs, and published in Heinrichs 2003–4, vol. LXXXVI, pp. 83–92, 88; Dr James Campbell suggests this seems to be the moment when the decision to rebuild the lantern in stone was taken (communication with the author, 2016), and that the visible settlement of the upper part of the structure reflects this change of stress.
37. Wren 1750, p. 343.
38. Ibid., p. 10.
39. Ibid.
40. Bendall et al. 1999, p. 275.
41. Shuckburgh 1904, p. 117.
42. Willis and Clark 1886, vol.1, p. 710.
43. Collinson 2006, p. 197.
44. Willis and Clark 1886, vol. II, p. 711.
45. Ibid., p. 708.
46. Stubbings 1977, p. 12.
47. Ibid.
48. Collinson 2006, p. 185.

49. Bendall et al. 1999, p. 275.
50. Ibid.
51. Rivers, 'Law, William (1686–1761)', ODNB, 2004.
52. Loggan 1690.
53. Willis and Clark 1886, vol. II, p. 717; RCHME 1959, p. 67.
54. Beddard, 'Sancroft, William (1617–1693)', ODNB, 2004; also see Collinson 2006, pp. 173–200.
55. Bendall et al. 1999, pp. 276–77.
56. Bertoloni Meli, 'Wallis, John (1616–1703)', ODNB, 2004, and see the biographical source cited in note 54 for Chapter 3, below.
57. See http://www-groups.dcs.st-and.ac.uk/history/Printonly/Wallis.html (accessed 30 July 2016).
58. See https://royalsociety.org/about-us/history (accessed 30 July 2016).
59. Ibid.
60. Bowden, 'Fane, Lady Rachael [married names Rachael Bourchier, countess of Bath; Rachael Cranfield, countess of Middlesex] (*bap.*1613, *d.*1680)', ODNB, 2005.
61. Ibid.
62. Willis and Clark 1886, vol. II, p. 717.
63. Hughes 1735, vol. I, p. 252.
64. Swift 1980 (1726).
65. Temple 1844, p. 547.

CHAPTER 4 · PAGES 83–101

1. Bendall et al. 1999, p. 294.
2. Winstanley 1935, p. 186.
3. Dyer 1814, vol. II, p. 344.
4. Mayor (ed.) 1911, pp. 166–99.
5. Bendall et al. 1999, p. 326.
6. Ibid., p. 322.
7. Ibid.
8. Willis and Clark 1886, vol. II, pp. 712–13.
9. Ibid., and the accounts were published by J.B. Peace in the *Emmanuel College Magazine* in 1898; for Lumley, see Colvin 2008, p. 665.
10. Peace 1898, pp. 86–88.
11. Willis and Clark 1886, vol. II, p. 713.
12. Peace 1898, pp. 86–88.
13. ECA: CHA.I.4.A, 'Admonition Book', 26b recto.
14. Ibid., 26a verso.
15. Colvin 2008, pp. 196–97.
16. Stubbings 1977, p. 14.
17. Wordsworth 1874, pp. 392–93.
18. Stubbings 1977, p. 14.
19. My thanks to Father Rob Mackley for the suggestion regarding the possible Eucharistic significance.
20. ECA: COL.14.2, fol. 19 verso.
21. Ibid.
22. Ibid.
23. London: British Library: Add Ms 42569, fol. 3 recto.
24. Jeremy Musson, 'Cambridge's hidden hall', *Country Life* (17 February 2016), pp. 62–66.
25. Thomas Cocke, 'James Essex', in Roderick Brown (ed.), *Architectural Outsiders* (London, 1985), pp. 98–113, p. 101. Dr Cocke's essay includes the fullest account of Essex's career, although it does not reference the particular set of drawings here discussed.
26. ECA: COL.14.2, fols 34–35.
27. ECA: COL.9.IB, Bennet's Book 1788, vol. II, p. 45.
28. Willis and Clark 1886, vol. IV, pp. 24–25.
29. Wordsworth 1874, pp. 392–93.
30. Ibid.
31. ECA: COL.14.2, fol. 66 verso.
32. Willis and Clark 1886, vol. III, p. 539.
33. Cocke 1985, pp. 109–10.
34. Ibid., p. 98.
35. ECA: COL.9.IB, Bennet's Book 1788, vol. II, p. 46.
36. Willis and Clark 1886, vol. II, p. 715.
37. Hartlebury: Hurd Library: 8 February 1771 letter sent out by William Richardson; for a version of the engraving, see ECA: PR.b.5.
38. Pevsner and Bradley 2014, pp. 74–75; the reference to Pembroke is made in Cocke 1985, p. 98. Dr Cocke suggests that Gibbs may have influenced Burrough's admiration of Wren, and that Burrough passed to Essex 'a respect for Wren unusual for the period'.
39. Bennet's Book 1788, vol. II, p. 46.
40. Campbell, 1716, vol. I, plates 3–6.
41. Ibid., plates 85–87.
42. Hartlebury: Hurd Library: letter from Richard Hurd, Archdeacon of Gloucester, to William Richardson, 14 February 1771.
43. Hartlebury: Hurd Library: letter from William Richardson to Richard Hurd, 16 February 1771.
44. Willis and Clark 1886, vol. II, p. 715.
45. Bennet's Book 1788, vol. II, p. 46.
46. Sherbo, 'Farmer, Richard (1735–1797)', ODNB, 2004.
47. Ibid.
48. Boswell 1811 (1791), p. 339.
49. Bendall et al. 1999, p. 399.
50. Gunning 1855, vol. I, p. 181.
51. Shuckburgh 1904, pp. 156–57.
52. Bendall et al. 1999, p. 398.
53. Helen Bradbury, 'Report on bathing pool', mss, 2016.
54. Bendall et al. 1999, pp. 397–98.
55. Sherbo, 'Farmer, Richard (1735–1797)', ODNB, 2004.
56. Stubbings 1983, no. 23.
57. Sherbo, 'Farmer, Richard (1735–1797)', ODNB, 2004.
58. Stubbings 1983, p. 23.
59. Gunning 1854, vol. I, pp. 178–79.
60. Cantor, 'Young, Thomas (1773–1829)', ODNB, 2004; Stubbings 1983, p. 33.
61. Stubbings 1983, p. 33.
62. Cantor, 'Young, Thomas (1773–1829)', ODNB, 2004.
63. Stubbings 1983, p. 33.

CHAPTER 5 · PAGES 103–27

1. Bendall et al. 1999, pp. 293–94.
2. Lysons and Lysons 1808, p. 29.
3. Ibid.; and ECA: Plans/NC/3–4.
4. Willis and Clark 1886, vol. II, p. 716.
5. Colvin 2008, pp. 555–56; ECA: COL.14.2, p. 183 verso, Order Book, 30 June 1824, Willis and Clark 1886, vol. II, p. 716.
6. ECA: Plans and elevation, July 1824/NC/3–4.
7. For the context of Soane's design for the plunge bath at Wimpole, near Cambridge, see http://collections.soane.org/SCHEME967 (accessed 4 August 2016).
8. Pevsner and Bradley 2014, pp. 26–27; Musson, 'Aesthetic attitudes', in Massing and Zeeman (eds) 2015, pp. 37–38.
9. ECA: Plan, 1811/FC.We.18; Peace 1898, pp. 83–95.
10. Bendall et al. 1999, p. 332; Order Book, 27 May 1828, COL.14.2, p. 196 recto.
11. Stubbings 1983, p. 32.
12. Ibid.
13. ECA: COL.14.3, p. 101.
14. Bendall et al. 1999, pp. 417.
15. Ibid., pp. 432–33.
16. Stubbings 1977, p. 16.
17. ECA: Em. Box 6, I.i, Alfred Waterhouse, December 1871.
18. Pevsner and Bradley 2014, p. 102; and for Girton, p. 99.
19. ECA: Em. Box 6, I.i, Alfred Waterhouse, letter 7 December 1871, to Master, fol. I verso/2 recto.
20. Ibid., fol. 3 recto.
21. Ibid.
22. Cunningham 1994, pp. 130–52.

23. This is my own observation, and cannot yet be related to any documentary evidence in the archives.
24. Stubbings 1977, p. 16.
25. Bendall et al. 1999, p. 510.
26. Ibid., p. 18.
27. Ibid., p. 20.
28. Stubbings 1977, p. 19.
29. Ibid., p. 20.
30. Bendall et al. 1999, pp. 512–13.
31. Shuckburgh 1904, opposite p. 188.
32. Pevsner and Bradley 2014, p. 94.
33. Willis and Clark 1886, vol. II, p. 717.
34. Bendall et al. 1999, p. 510.
35. Willis and Clark 1886, vol. II, p. 718.
36. Butler 2013.
37. Willis and Clark 1886, vol. II, p. 718; vol. IV, pp. 24–25.
38. Easton 1984, p. 3, a memoir of a Master's daughter, which includes a plan of the lost Lodge and an account of life in the Lodge.
39. Shuckburgh 1904, pp. 183–84.
40. Bendall et al. 1999, pp. 512–13.
41. ECA: Plans and elevations, 1885/HOS/2–4.
42. *The Building News* (30 July 1880) illustrates the new King's College choir school designed by Fawcett; *The Building News* (15 July 1881) illustrates his design for the house for the curator of the Botanic Gardens in Cambridge.
43. ECA: Plans and elevations, 1885/HOS/2–4.
44. Bendall et al. 1999, pp. 512–13; ECA: Plans, 1891/HOS/40–44, gives plans and elevation but they appear to be only a poor tracing.
45. Waterhouse, 'Pearson, John Loughborough (1817–1897)', rev. Anthony Quiney, *ODNB*, 2004.
46. Pevsner and Bradley 2014, p. 247.
47. Bendall et al. 1999, p. 513.
48. Pevsner and Bradley 2014, p. 346.
49. ECA: Em.27, reports on potential sports grounds in the 1890s, and correspondence over the design of the pavilion.
50. ECA: Plans, 1933/SQ/1–2.
51. Anon., *Emmanuel College Magazine*, vol. I (1 May 1889), pp. 28–36, and vol. II (October 1889), pp. 72–80.
52. ECA: Rachel Wroth, 'Emmanuel College servants in the 19th century', typescript, 2001, pp. 1–2.
53. Barham 1986, pp. 1–2.
54. Shuckburgh 1904, p. 185.
55. Bendall et al. 1999, p. 420.
56. Ibid., pp. 417–20.
57. See http://www.emma.cam.ac.uk/about/history/masters/?id=16 (accessed 20 July 2016).
58. Brooke 1993, vol. IV, p. 58.
59. Bendall et al. 1999, p. 420.
60. Dale, 'Hopkins, Sir Frederick Gowland (1861–1947)', *ODNB*, 2004.
61. See http://www.nobelprize.org/nobel_prizes/medicine/laureates/1929/hopkins-bio.html (accessed 20 July 2016).
62. Ibid.

CHAPTER 6 · PAGES 129–65

1. Bendall et al. 1999, pp. 566–68.
2. This collaborative approach prompted the Conservation Statement review by Cambridge Architectural Research Ltd (CAR Ltd) submitted in early 2016, of which the author of this book was a co-principal.
3. Shuckburgh 1904, p. 185.
4. Bendall et al. 1999, pp. 513–14; ECA: Em.12.41, by architect J.W. Simpson.
5. Molesworth Roberts 1946, pp. 173–76, 173; see also Ward 2009.
6. Molesworth Roberts 1946, p. 173.
7. Ward 2009, pp. 123–25.
8. Ibid., pp. 129–31.
9. Bendall et al. 1999, p. 515.
10. ECA: Plans/LIB/1–12.
11. Bendall et al 1999, p. 516, Pevsner and Bradley 2014, p. 94; ECA: Plans/NthC/1–21, 100–3.
12. Ward 2009, p. 135.
13. Ibid., pp. 118–20.
14. ECA: Plans/NthC/1–21, 100–3.
15. Ward 2009, pp. 134–35.
16. See https://www.emma.cam.ac.uk/about/history/ww1 (accessed 20 July 2016).
17. Anon., 'War memorial', *Emmanuel College Magazine*, vol. XXII (1919–20), p. 42.
18. ECA: COL.13.12.
19. Bendall et al. 1999, p. 516–17; Pevsner and Bradley 2014, p. 94; Ward 2009, p. 132.
20. ECA: Plans, 1955–1962/KB/6–30; and Fawcett 2012, pp. 1–14; and additional information and research shared by William Fawcett, including email correspondence with, and copies of drawings from, Mr Begg.
21. Fawcett, ibid.
22. Bendall et al. 1999, p. 519.
23. Stamp 2013, pp. 8–9.
24. *Cambridge Daily News* (2 March 1959).
25. Stamp 2013, p. 9.
26. Bendall et al. 1999, p. 519.
27. Lord St John of Fawsley, 1993, pp. 130–33; ECA: MAS.8.1.1.
28. ECA: Em.28.115a, letter from Hon. Vita Sackville-West to David Woollam, 5 October 1960; also Codrington's sketch designs, Em.28, 116.
29. Bendall et al. 1999, p. 520.
30. Ibid.
31. ECA: Plans, 1963–4/SC/1–123, for interiors of bedsits, SC/11a and b.
32. http://www.hopkins.co.uk (accessed 29 December 2016).
33. ECA: Plans, elevations and section, 1993–1995/QB/1–194; and interview with Sir Michael Hopkins by the author in 2015, for the CAR Ltd Conservation Statement (CS), http://www.hopkins.co.uk/projects/2/76 (accessed 10 August 2016).
34. Correspondence with the author, 2016, and see Burgoyne 1993–94, vol. lxxvi, pp. 117–22.
35. Interview with Sir Michael Hopkins by the author, 2015, http://www.hopkins.co.uk/projects/current/204 (accessed 10 August 2016).
36. Pesvner and Bradley 2014, p. 94; and information from Dr Mike Gross, Bursar, 2015.
37. Pesvner and Bradley 2014, p. 94.
38. Ibid.
39. Inskip 2004–5, vol. lxxxvii, pp. 55–83.
40. 2016 student survey for the CAR Ltd CS.
41. Sealy and Gray 1996.
42. Advice from garden historian, Tim Richardson, 2015.
43. Sealy and Gray 1996, pp. 11–12.
44. Ibid.
45. Bendall et al. 1999, pp. 548–51.
46. Stubbings 1983, p. 49.
47. Ibid.
48. See http://www.nobelprize.org/nobel_prizes/chemistry/laureates/1967 (accessed 11 September 2016).
49. Stubbings 1983, p. 48.
50. See http://www.nobelprize.org/nobel_prizes/chemistry/laureates/1967/porter-facts.html (accessed 11 September 2016).

Picture Credits

p. 8: © Marcus Ginns

pp. 22–23, 25, 88: © British Library Board. All Rights Reserved/Bridgeman Images

p. 24: by kind permission of Michael H. Peters

p. 26: © Jon Harris

p. 27: © Getty Images

p. 28: © The Hamilton Kerr Institute, University of Cambridge

p. 29: © Museum Catharijneconvent, Utrecht (ABM S71)

p. 32: © by kind permission of the Syndics of Cambridge University Library, SS12.1.item 7

pp. 33, 34, 36, 37, 38, 40, 43, 48, 49, 50, 52, 53, 56, 58, 60, 61, 65, 72, 74–75, 76, 77, 78–79, 80, 81 (right), 92, 94, 100, 101, 104, 105 (left), 106, 109, 110, 111, 114, 115, 118, 119, 125, 126, 134, 135, 142: by kind permission of the Master and Fellows of Emmanuel College Cambridge

p. 39: © The Bodleian Libraries, The University of Oxford, Hamond map of Cambridge 1592

p. 45: Photo © Granger/Bridgeman Images

p. 57: © by kind permission of the Syndics of Cambridge University Library, Maps bb.53.63.1

p. 59: © The National Portrait Gallery, London

p. 64: © The Warden and Fellows of All Souls College Oxford

p. 81 (left): Private collection

p. 89: by kind permission of The Master and Fellows of Trinity Hall Cambridge

p. 93 (above): by kind permission of The Master, Fellows and Scholars of Downing College Cambridge

pp. 93 (below), 98: © Christine Penney; reproduced by kind permission of the Bishop of Worcester and the Church Commissioners

pp. 122 (left), 130: © The Royal Institute of British Architects

p. 122 (right): © reproduced by permission of Historic England Archive

p. 127: © Bernard Dunstan

pp. 137: © Cambridgeshire Collection, Cambridge Central Library

pp. 149, 151: © by kind permission of Bella Hancock; images held in the Emmanuel College Archives

p. 152 (below): © Hopkins Architects

pp. 154, 155: © Dennis Gilbert/VIEW

p. 165 (right): © Susan Ryder

pp. 178–79: © The Master and Fellows of Emmanuel College Cambridge; illustration by Lee Marshall

Author photograph on jacket flap: © Daren Fentiman

SVRSVM COR

Select Bibliography

TONY BAGGS, *Cambridge 1574–1904. A Portfolio of Twelve Maps Illustrating the Changing Plan of Cambridge* (Cambridge, 2002), Cambridgeshire Records Society, vol. XVII

JANE BARHAM, *Backstairs Cambridge* (Orwell, Herts, 1986)

SARAH BENDALL, CHRISTOPHER BROOKE AND PATRICK COLLINSON, *A History of Emmanuel College, Cambridge* (Woodbridge, 1999)

FRANCIS BLOMEFIELD, *Collectanea Cantabrigiensia, or Collections Relating to Cambridge* (Norwich, 1751)

A.T. BOLTON AND H. DUNCAN HENDRY (eds), 'Designs and drawings by Sir Christopher Wren for St Paul's Cathedral, the Residentiaries' houses, and the Deanery', *Wren Society*, vol. XIII (1936), pp. 51–55

JAMES BOSWELL, *The Life of Samuel Johnson* (London, 1811; first published 1791)

DEREK BREWER, 'Bowls', *Emmanuel College Magazine*, Quatercentenary issue (1984), pp. 43–46

CHRISTOPHER BROOKE, *History of the University of Cambridge* (Cambridge, 1993), vol. IV

CHRIS BURGOYNE, 'How does the new building stand up?', *Emmanuel College Magazine*, vol. LXXXVI (1993–94), pp. 117–22

RICHARD BUTLER, *Secular & Domestic: George Gilbert Scott and the Master's Lodge of St John's College* (Cambridge, 2013)

COLEN CAMPBELL, *Vitruvius Britannicus* (London, 1716), vol. I

THOMAS COCKE, 'James Essex', in Roderick Brown (ed.), *Architectural Outsiders* (London, 1985), pp. 98–113

PATRICK COLLINSON, *From Cranmer to Sancroft* (London, 2006)

HOWARD COLVIN, *A Biographical Dictionary of British Architects, 1600–1840* (New Haven and London, 2008), p. 1159.

COLIN CUNNINGHAM, 'Practicality and preservation: Alfred Waterhouse and the Cambridge colleges', *Architectural History*, vol. 37 (1994), pp. 130–52

KERRY DOWNES, *The Architecture of Wren* (London, 1982)

GEORGE DYER, *History of the University and Colleges of Cambridge Including Notices of the Founders and Eminent Men* (London, 1814), vol. II

C.P. EASTON, *A Few Memories* (Cambridge, 1984)

WILLIAM FAWCETT, 'The post-World War II traditionalists in Oxbridge', 2012 draft paper, pp. 1–14; an edited version of this paper was published in *Oxford & Cambridge*, vol. 11 of the annual *Twentieth Century Architecture*, published by the Twentieth Century Society, 2013

JONATHAN FOYLE, 'Is this the earliest known portrait of an English artisan?', *Financial Times* (24 March 2016)

Detail of the reredos in the Chapel, the gift of William Sancroft to his old College, on the eve of his ejection from office as Archbishop of Canterbury following the accession of William III and Mary II.

THOMAS FULLER, *The History of the University, ... to 1634* (Cambridge, 1840)

VIKTOR FÜRST, *The Architecture of Sir Christopher Wren* (London, 1956)

ANTONY GERAGHTY, *The Architectural Drawings of Sir Christopher Wren at All Souls College Oxford: A Complete Catalogue* (New Haven and London, 2007)

ANTHONY GERAGHTY, *The Sheldonian Theatre: Architecture and Learning in Seventeenth-Century Oxford* (New Haven and London, 2013)

A.V. GRIMSTONE, *Building Pembroke Chapel: Wren, Pearce and Scott* (Cambridge, 2009)

WALTER GUMBLEY, *The Cambridge Dominicans* (Oxford, 1938)

HENRY GUNNING, *Reminiscences of the University, Town, and County of Cambridge, from the Year 1780* (London, 1855), vol. I

JOHANNA HEINRICHS, 'Wren and the Chapel reviewed', *Emmanuel College Magazine*, vol. LXXXVI (2003–4), pp. 83–92

JOHN HUGHES, *Poems of Several Occasions* (London, 1735), vol. I

PETER INSKIP, 'Emmanuel College Chapel: reordering via restoration', *Emmanuel College Magazine*, vol. LXXXVII (2004–5), pp. 55–83

LISA JARDINE, *On a Grander Scale: the Outstanding Career of Sir Christopher Wren* (London, 2002)

NORMAN JONES, *Governing by Virtue* (Oxford, 2015)

STANFORD. E. LEHMBERG, *Sir Walter Mildmay and Tudor Government* (Austin, TX, 1964)

DAVID LOGGAN, *Cantabrigia Illustrata* (Cambridge, 1690; reprint 1905)

DANIEL AND SAMUEL LYSONS, *Magna Britannia: Cambridgeshire* (London, 1808)

JOHN MAYOR (ed.), *Cambridge under Queen Anne, Cambridge* (Cambridge, 1911)

H.V. MOLESWORTH ROBERTS, 'Leonard Aloysius Stokes', *Architectural Review*, vol. 100 (1946), pp. 173–76

JEREMY MUSSON, 'Aesthetic attitudes', in J.-M. Massing and N. Zeeman (eds), *King's College Chapel 1515–2015: Art, Music and Religion in Cambridge* (London, 2015), pp. 37–38

JEREMY MUSSON, '"Below envy, but above contempt": the Deanery House at St Paul's Cathedral, London', *Georgian Group Journal* (forthcoming 2017)

J.B. PEACE, 'The College buildings in the eighteenth century', *Emmanuel College Magazine*, vol. IX (Lent Term, 1898), p. 88

NIKOLAUS PEVSNER AND SIMON BRADLEY, *Buildings of England: Cambridgeshire* (New Haven and London, 2014)

TIM RAWLE, *Cambridge* (London, 2005)

NICHOLAS ROGERS, 'The provenance of the Thornham Parva retable', in N. Rogers (ed.), *Harlaxton Medieval Studies, XIX, The Friars in Medieval Britain* (Donington, 2010), pp. 185–93.

ROYAL COMMISSION ON THE HISTORICAL MONUMENTS OF ENGLAND (RCHME), *An Inventory of the Historical Monuments in the City of Cambridge* (London, 1959)

GORDON RUPP, 'Sir Walter Mildmay', *Emmanuel College Magazine*, Quatercentenary issue (1984), pp. 24–27

LORD ST JOHN OF FAWSLEY, 'The Master's Lodge', *House and Garden* (June 1993), pp. 130–33

L.F. SALZMAN (ed.), *A History of the County of Cambridge and the Isle of Ely* (London, 1948), vol. II

WOLFGANG SCHENLUHN, *Architektur de Betterlorden* (Darmstadt, 2000)

GEORGE SEALY AND RON GRAY, *Emmanuel College Buildings and Gardens* (Cambridge, 1996)

EDUARD F. SECKLER, *Wren and his Place in European Architecture* (London, 1954)

E.S. SHUCKBURGH, *Laurence Chaderton DD Translated from a Latin Memoir of Dr Dillingham* (Cambridge, 1884; first published in Latin in 1700)

E.S. SHUCKBURGH, 'Emmanuel worthies: the founder and the first Master', *Emmanuel College Magazine*, vol. I (May 1889), pp. 9–19, 18

E.S. SHUCKBURGH, *Emmanuel College* (London, 1904)

DAVID SOUDEN, 'Restoration of the Gallery', *Emmanuel College Magazine*, Quatercentenary issue (1984), pp. 56–60

GAVIN STAMP, *Anti-Ugly: Excursions in English Architecture and Design* (London, 2013)

FRANK STUBBINGS, 'The church of the Cambridge Dominicans', *Proceedings of the Cambridge Antiquarian Society*, vol. lxii (January 1969–December 1969), pp. 94–104

FRANK STUBBINGS, *Emmanuel College Chapel: 1677–1977* (Cambridge, 1977)

FRANK STUBBINGS, *Forty-Nine Lives: an Anthology of Portraits of Emmanuel Men* (Cambridge, 1983)

FRANK STUBBINGS, 'The College charter', *Emmanuel College Magazine*, vol. LXXII (1989–90), p. 29

FRANK STUBBINGS, *The Statutes of Sir Walter Mildmay for Emmanuel College* (Cambridge, 2005)

JONATHAN SWIFT, *Gulliver's Travels* (London, 1980, with notes by Michael Foot; first published 1726)

TIM TATTON-BROWN, *Lambeth Palace: a History of the Archbishops of Canterbury and their Houses* (London, 2000), pp. 79–80

SIR WILLIAM TEMPLE, *The Works of Sir William Temple* (London, 1740 and 1844), 2 vols

ADRIAN TINNISWOOD, *His Invention So Fertile: a Life of Christopher Wren* (London, 2002)

JOHN TWIGG, *A History of Queens' College, Cambridge (1448–1986)* (London, 1986)

JAN WARD, *The Leonard Stokes Directory: Architect in a Dressing Gown* (Jan Ward, 2009)

MARGARET WHINNEY, *Wren* (London, 1970)

ROBERT WILLIS AND JOHN WILLIS CLARK, *The Architectural History of the University of Cambridge and of the Colleges of Cambridge* (Cambridge, 1886), 4 vols

DAVID WINSTANLEY, *Unreformed Cambridge* (Cambridge, 1935)

R.C. WINTHROP, *Life and Letters of John Winthrop* (Boston, 1864), vol. I

CHRISTOPHER WORDSWORTH, *Social Life at English Universities in the Eighteenth Century* (Cambridge, 1874)

CHRISTOPHER WREN, *Parentalia: or Memoirs of the Family of the Wrens: viz. Mathew, Bishop of Ely, Christopher, Dean of Windsor &c. but Most Chiefly of Sir Christopher Wren, Late Surveyor-General of the Royal Buildings* ... (London, 1750)

P.R. ZUTSHI (ed.), *The Dominicans in Cambridge 1238–1538: a Catalogue of a Commemorative Exhibition* (Cambridge, 1988)

PATRICK ZUTSHI AND ROBERT OMBRES OP, 'The Dominicans in Cambridge 1238–1538', *Archivum Fratrum Praedicatorum*, vol. LX (1990), pp. 313–73.

REPORTS:

ALISON DICKENS, 'Archaeological Observations at Emmanuel College Kitchens', *Cambridge Archaeological Unit (CAU)* Report no. 55 (Cambridge, 1992)

ALISON DICKENS, 'An Archaeological Assessment at The Master's Lodge Forecourt, Emmanuel College, Cambridge' *CAU* Report no. 81 (Cambridge, 1993)

ALISON DICKENS, 'Archaeological Excavations in The Master's Lodge Forecourt, Emmanuel College, Cambridge', *CAU* Report no. 110 (Cambridge, 1994)

ODNB ONLINE:

R.A.P.J. BEDDARD, 'Sancroft, William (1617–1693)', *Oxford Dictionary of National Biography* (Oxford, 2004), http://www.oxforddnb.com.ezproxy2.londonlibrary.co.uk/view/article/24610 (accessed 10 August 2016)

DOMENICO BERTOLONI MELI, 'Wallis, John (1616–1703)', *Oxford Dictionary of National Biography* (Oxford, 2004), http://www.oxforddnb.com.ezproxy2.londonlibrary.co.uk/view/article/28572 (accessed 10 August 2016)

CAROLINE M.K. BOWDEN, 'Fane, Lady Rachael [married names Rachael Bourchier, countess of Bath; Rachael Cranfield, countess of Middlesex] (*bap.*1613, *d.*1680)', *Oxford Dictionary of National Biography* (Oxford, 2004), http://www.oxforddnb.com.ezproxy2.londonlibrary.co.uk/view/article/93575 (accessed 10 August 2016)

GEOFFREY CANTOR, 'Young, Thomas (1773–1829)', *Oxford Dictionary of National Biography* (Oxford, 2004), http://www.oxforddnb.com.ezproxy2.londonlibrary.co.uk/view/article/30282 (accessed 10 August 2016)

T.H. COCKE, 'Essex, James (*bap.*1722, *d.*1784)', *Oxford Dictionary of National Biography* (Oxford, 2004), http://www.oxforddnb.com.ezproxy2.londonlibrary.co.uk/view/article/8887 (accessed 14 August 2016)

PATRICK COLLINSON, 'Chaderton, Laurence (1536?–1640)', *Oxford Dictionary of National Biography* (Oxford, 2004), http://www.oxforddnb.com.ezproxy2.londonlibrary.co.uk/view/article/5010 (accessed 14 August 2016).

H.H. DALE, 'Hopkins, Sir Frederick Gowland (1861–1947)', *Oxford Dictionary of National Biography* (Oxford, 2004), http://www.oxforddnb.com.ezproxy2.londonlibrary.co.uk/view/article/33977 (accessed 10 August 2016)

L.L. FORD, 'Mildmay, Sir Walter (1520/21–1589)', *Oxford Dictionary of National Biography* (Oxford, 2004), http://www.oxforddnb.com.ezproxy2.londonlibrary.co.uk/view/article/18696 (accessed 10 August 2016)

ISABEL RIVERS, 'Law, William (1686–1761)', *Oxford Dictionary of National Biography* (Oxford, 2004), http://www.oxforddnb.com.ezproxy2.londonlibrary.co.uk/view/article/16154 (accessed 10 August 2016)

ARTHUR SHERBO, 'Farmer, Richard (1735–1797)', *Oxford Dictionary of National Biography* (Oxford, 2004), http://www.oxforddnb.com.ezproxy2.londonlibrary.co.uk/view/article/9169 (accessed 10 August 2016)

PAUL WATERHOUSE, 'Pearson, John Loughborough (1817–1897)', rev. Anthony Quiney, *Oxford Dictionary of National Biography* (Oxford, 2004), http://www.oxforddnb.com.ezproxy2.londonlibrary.co.uk/view/article/21720 (accessed 10 August 2016)

STEPHEN WRIGHT, 'Frankland, Joyce (1531–1587)', *Oxford Dictionary of National Biography* (Oxford, 2004), http://www.oxforddnb.com.ezproxy2.londonlibrary.co.uk/view/article/10084 (accessed 10 August 2016)

The Buildings and Grounds of Emmanuel College Cambridge

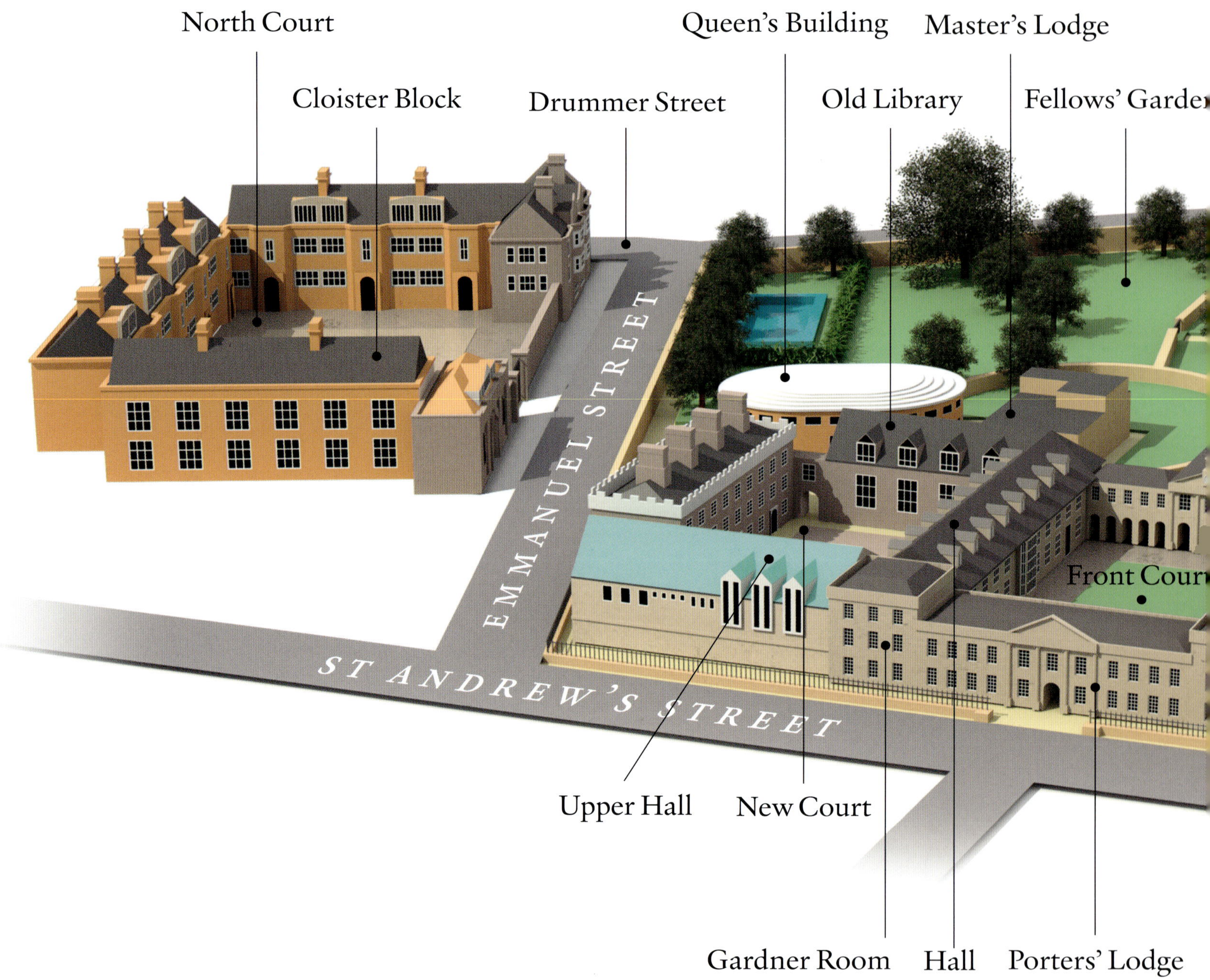

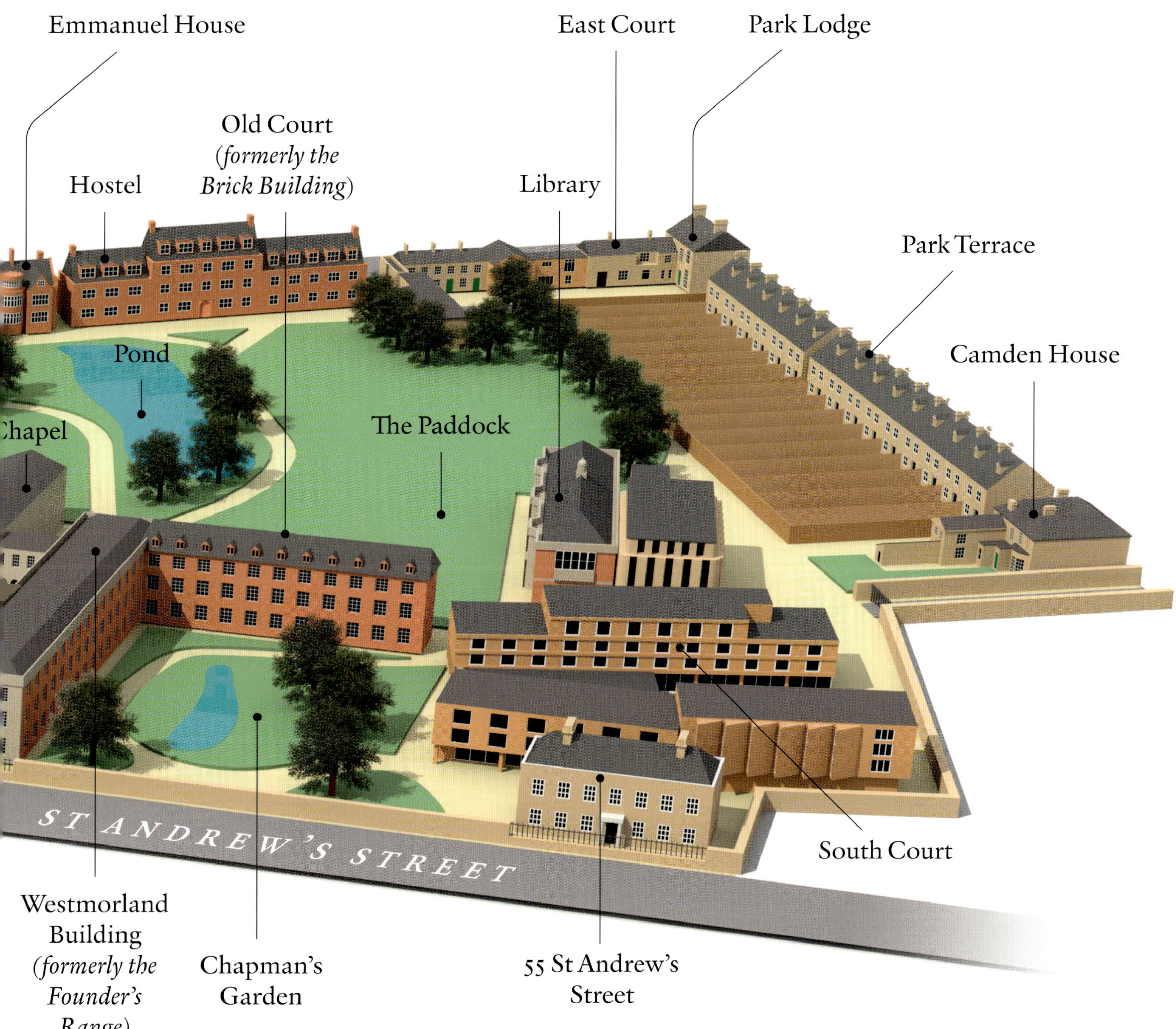
Emmanuel House
East Court
Park Lodge
Old Court
(formerly the
Brick Building)
Hostel
Library
Park Terrace
Pond
Camden House
hapel
The Paddock
ST ANDREW'S STREET
South Court
Westmorland
Building
(formerly the
Founder's
Range)
Chapman's
Garden
55 St Andrew's
Street

strenuus et fidelis 35
Margareta Concionator 21
ademiæ Regiſtrarius 20
Per Annos.
nibus officiis ita perfunctus est,
ullum hujuſce ſæculi virum
ut vivum magis coluerit,
Aut mortuum defleverit
Academia.
Obiit 23º Januarii.
A. D. 1778.
Ætat. 70.

Acknowledgements

First and foremost I must thank the Master, Dame Fiona Reynolds, and the Fellows of Emmanuel, for inviting me to write this architectural history, the first illustrated survey of the College's building on this scale. This followed a conservation review that I led for Cambridge Architectural History Research Ltd, working closely with Oliver Caroe, Jon Harris and Eleanor Rule. Sarah Bendall, Fellow Librarian, has been exceptionally generous with her support, reading and re-reading the text and improving it. Amanda Goode, College Archivist, has also been endlessly patient in helping me to solve questions and queries, and Helen Carron, College Librarian, kindly gave me access to the draft catalogue of Sancroft's library. Mike Gross, Bursar, Robert Henderson, Senior Tutor, and Barry Windeatt, Vice-Master and Keeper of Special Collections, have given the project valuable support. Nigel Spivey, Fellow, and Andrew Fane, President of the Emmanuel Society, gave constructive thoughts on the early text.

This book will be remembered for Will Pryce's outstanding photography; it is a pleasure to work with a photographer so interested in architecture. We are similarly fortunate in our talented designer Robert Dalrymple, who read the text closely and visited the College with me to understand fully his task, and produced these elegant pages. Nigel Luckhurst did an excellent job photographing archival images and paintings in the College. I am also immensely grateful to the patient and rigorous Scala editors, Coralie Hepburn and Linda Schofield, and to Harriet Salisbury who read and improved the first draft.

Architectural historians James Campbell, Anthony Geraghty, Richard Hewlings, Alan Powers, Frank Salmon and Gavin Stamp all gave helpful advice, as did Donal Cooper, John Maddison and Hugh Richmond. Artist and architectural historian Jon Harris brought much thought and talent to the reconstruction drawing of the Cambridge Black Friars' House. Tim Richardson also gave me an interesting insight into the gardens of Emmanuel.

I am grateful to the many archivists and librarians who make this sort of project possible, particularly those of the Cambridge University Library, British Library and London Library, as well as Gaye Morgan at All Souls Oxford; Chris Penney at the Hurd Library, Hartlebury Castle, Worcestershire; Dominique Ruhlman, Alexandra Browne and John Pollard of Trinity Hall Cambridge; and Karen Lubarr of Downing College Cambridge. I also thank Jan Relf and Bella Hancock for advice on Tom Hancock's drawings, Sir Michael and Lady Hopkins, Hannah Dickerson and Nathaniel Moore of Hopkins Architects for help on the Queen's Building, and Chris Burgoyne of Emmanuel for his concise explanation of the engineering.

Many people at Emmanuel College – Fellows, staff and students – have been helpful and supportive in different ways. I particularly thank the Dean, Jeremy Caddick, who kindly arranged for a full lighting set-up of the Chapel to record that extraordinary space lit for evensong, and to Francesco Cusimano for the early laying up of the Hall, Parlour and Gallery for special dinners, so they could be recorded for this book, on what were already very busy days; thanks too to the porters team, the Buildings Manager David Hobbs and the team in the maintenance department, Head Gardener Christoph Keate and his fellow gardeners, and many others, who were all courteous and welcoming to myself as a regular visitor full of questions and often in need of keys. I also thank my wife, Sophie, and daughters, Georgia and Miranda, for their companionship and patience with all my writing projects.

JEREMY MUSSON, 2017

Detail of a late eighteenth-century memorial in the Cloister.

Index

Illustrations are shown in *italics*.